A
ROAD TRANSPORT
HERITAGE

VOLUME II

BOB TUCK

Published by Bob Tuck
Low Worsall, Yarm,
Cleveland. England. TS15 9QA

ISBN 0 9521938 1 7

First Published 1994

copyright 1994 Bob Tuck

Other Books by Bob Tuck

Moving Mountains
Mountain Movers
Mammoth Trucks
Hauling Heavyweights
The Supertrucks of Scammell
Move It (compendium of *Moving Mountains*
and *Mountain Movers*)
Carrying Cargo
Classic Hauliers
Robsons
Classic Hauliers 2
The Golden Days of Heavy Haulage
A Road Transport Heritage

Printed in Great Britain by
The Amadeus Press Ltd
Huddersfield, West Yorkshire

Typesetting by Highlight Type Bureau Ltd
Shipley, West Yorkshire.

CONTENTS

Front cover - Ken Thomas

From modest beginnings, the Ken Thomas fleet from Guyhirn are now a distinctive sight in all parts of the UK mainland. H97 UBD was one of 12 Scanias being operated in early 1994, the 6x2 tag axle unit being usually driven by Les Crow. Les joined the firm in 1978 and was given this Scania when new. When photographed by David Fairbrother, the immaculate 113-320 had covered more than 520,000 kms. Pictured coupled to a Nene 13.6 metre semi-trailer which incorporates air suspension, a self tracking rearmost axle and Laurence David curtainsider bodywork, Les would usually be engaged in delivering palleted foodstuffs. Reflecting the company's diverse interests, the Scania is also used to haul refrigerated semi-trailer vans as well as potato bulkers. Collecting produce from the field is still an important activity for Thomas' in the 1990s just as it was when Ken began in haulage during 1948.

Rear cover - W&J Riding

Those who've followed the long run of W&J Ridings may have spotted two different additions to the company's livery over the years. When the company opened a depot in South Bank (now in Cleveland but then in North Yorkshire) in the mid 1950s, the white and red roses circled by a belt was added to illustrate how Riding's services from Longridge in Lancashire were joining the two rose counties together. About 1976, Ridings began personalising each tractor unit with a door mounted name and reflecting the family's passion for steam, all the vehicles were named after rail locomotives. Rather fittingly F500 BFV, which was the company's first lightweight Seddon Atkinson Strato with L10-325 engine, received the name 'Invincible'. This was the first name ever to be allocated and originally used on AMS 113K, a second hand Atkinson Borderer which came to Ridings from Monklands of Coatbridge. Regular driver of the new fleet number 24 was Reg Nuttall, his vehicle being pictured by Alan Watts in the ICI Hillhouse works near Blackpool discharging pvc powder from a Carmichael 58 cu.metre tipping tank by means of an Edbro single mounted ram.

Front and rear end montages

Sid Milne was to drive for both Baxters and Northumbrian Transport before he found himself nationalised to become a small cog of BRS. Although his son Geoff wasn't to follow him into a driving life, he did inherit Sid's interest in transport. That passion is perhaps even stronger after more than 30 years as a national fleet enthusiast although Geoff's early photographs reflect his roots on Tyneside. West Street car park in Gateshead was a good night time spotting point as was the nearby Team Valley Trading Estate. Teams regularly used to host the local lorry driver of the year competitions although an early ride to Edinburgh also recorded similar activity. Geoff's wide interest in the late 1960s is reflected with some vehicles pictured at the Hoppings - Newcastle's big showman's event held every year on the Town Moor.

Title page - St Ives Sand & Gravel

Perhaps the most faithful servant in the extensive St Ives fleet was 185 EEW which came new into service during 1962. Seen hauling a 60' long hollow beam destined for the ever growing M1 motorway, all up weight is about 35 tons. In 1966 the vehicle was totally refurbished and was set for another 10 years of life with regular driver Alan Huggins before it's leisurely top speed of 34mph saw it pensioned off. The other long serving Foden S20 at St Ives was 934 CEW which was normally driven by Frank Mott - known as the master of towing as he could literally handle anything.

ACKNOWLEDGEMENTS

It's always a great support knowing there's many fellow transport followers who give without question time and help in putting my books together. Those in particular who have assisted with photographs for this volume are: Paul Adams, Robert Bate, Kenny Borland, Dick Bradbeer, Martin Brown, Peter, Chip & Geoff Burn, Les Christian, Ethel and Harry Clark, Norman Cleave, Donald Cook, John Curwen, Derek Freeland, David Fyldes, Norman & Alan Graham, Chris Herring, Barrie Hindmarch, Steve & Charles Hoggarth, Peter Johnson, Pat Kane, Les Kirman, Jim Lane, Alf Leadbetter, Ian Manship, Donald McGillivray, George Morris, James Munton, Bill Mustard, John & Peter Nicholson, Don Parkin, Sandy Reive, Jack Richards, Tom Riding, Sam Rudd, David Spowart, John Thomas, Bob Winter and Ted Yardley with particular thanks to Phil Sampson for providing the cover photograph.

Of equal importance are those who have helped with information to make the captions of more interest and these include: Graham Adams, Nicky Armstrong, Don Bewick, Bill Dey, Henry Dunmore, Peter East, Leonard Green, Dave Hawkins, Jack Martin, Chris Miller, Andy Robson and David Rowland.

Once again the assistance of Roger and Betty Kenny merit a special mention as does the long term support by my wife Sylvia. However I cannot pass without making reference to George Baker, Alan Martin and Malcolm Wilford whose knowledge in their own particular fields never ceases to amaze me.

AUTHOR'S PREFACE

It may come as no suprise that A Road Transport Heritage Volume 2 follows the pattern laid down by it's predecessor. Many found the first volume to be of interest although one of the slight criticisms levelled related to omissions.

Even though the UK is based on a relatively small collection of islands, the wealth of our transport history is massive. With such a choice, it's natural however, we all have specific hauliers or regions of the country which may be of more interest than others. I'm conscious that my selection of more than 40 hauliers for coverage may not satisfy every reader but all I ask is you give me time.

Due to the assistance of many people I've endeavoured to feature a larger geographical spread than the first volume without loosing any of the earlier variety. I should stress that I'm always amenable to suggestions or offers of help, as all being well further volumes of 'Heritage' should be possible.

Pictured about 1937, the Adams fleet is seen at the rear of Alice's cottage in Hilton Lane, Shareshill which is just north of Wolverhampton. George Adams is at the helm of Bedford DDH 325 with mate Ray Worsey sat at the front wheel. Walter Scott is pictured in the centre Morris 3 tonner JW 6856 with Charlie Adams in the Bedford ADA 368. The figure on the far right is Alf Powis who later became Mayor of Blackpool. With 'Burn Hollybank Coals' written on one side of the Bedford tipper, 'Use Hilton Bricks' is painted on the other side as an indication of Adams' two main customers. The site of Hilton Main colliery is now taken up by Wolverhampton's BP Truckstop.

When Fred Adams was killed in a mining accident down Hilton Main Colliery in 1932, his wife Alice decided to buy a lorry with the insurance and set her two sons - George and Charlie - up in transport. The Prudential pay out was £100 and for £90, the tax, insurance and deposit on a petrol engined Chevrolet two tonner registration ADH 55 was paid. Hilton Main was to provide the first work for the brothers and George Adams recalls for their first day's haulage, they earned nearly £2. Although he was the younger at 17, George was the only brother who could drive at the time so until his kid brother showed him how to handle a tipper, 20 year old Charlie rode in the Chevy's passenger seat. This Anthony Hoist equipped International came a few years on, it being bought new from a Mr Fox of Stoke-on-Trent in 1936.

With the two Adams brothers being required to serve elsewhere during the war, the transport company was put into limbo. In 1945 it was business as usual with Bedfords again being favoured, two of them being GXF 620 and JJW 736. In 1955, 720 FRE, the first of many new Leylands came from Charlie Ferry of Brownhills Motor Sales, it being soon followed by similar Leyland four wheelers 429 & 430 KRE. NNR 301 was a six wheeled Comet with a Boys trailing axle which was used on coke work and 6585 E was a Comet four wheeler which came in 1961. Adams were to go into skip hire during the 1970s, the waste transport fleet - which peaked around the 50 mark - being sold to BFI in 1986. John Adams, grandson of Alice Adams, now runs about 11 tippers on bulk haulage work from Cannock still under the A Adams title.

New Malden in Surrey has seen activity in road haulage by several generations of Adams' back as far as the mid 1920s. Nationalisation wiped out many of these concerns including Adams Bros (Super Transport) Ltd which became British Transport Commission Unit No A138. Graham Adams - under the slogan of Adams Super Service - was established in 1954 and their speciality if anything, has always been the unusual. Rated as a 25 tonner, 5 EPL is engaged in a cross European haul which saw this 18 ton pressure vessel delivered from Germany to Cwbran in South Wales. Vic Brice is the driver climbing aboard, the Gardner 6LW powered unit - which dates from 1958 - needing only 5 ton of ballast to haul this 70' long load.

At 24 ton in weight, this Bronx Press Brake was transported from Park Royal in London to Plymouth on behalf of Remington Rand. What made the load special was what happened after driver Des Davey reached the south west. The machine had to come off the rear of the Taskers semi-trailer so the four in line wheels were first removed. However as there was a bank approximately 3' 6" high to negotiate, the tractor was unhitched and the whole loaded trailer was jacked up to clear the obstacle before winching the 24 ton lump off. Rated as a 25 tonner, the Foden S21 dates from 1959. It's spec' included a Gardner 6LX-150 engine and 12 speed gearbox.

Seddons have always figured strongly in the Graham Adams fleet line up with the Cummins powered 250 RPD being the company's most famous example. It was this tractor unit which hauled Donald Campbell's 'Bluebird' to the Utah Salt Flats in the USA for his attempt on the world land speed record. Closer to home is FPJ 601C which is hauling the yacht 'Bandola' on behalf of it's owner Mr Graham Wood. The 5 ton boat was built by RJ Pryor of Burnham on Crouch and Adams transported it to Godalming. The wide supporting cradle allowed the boat to be jacked up prior to removing the Taskers 'Little Giant' semi-trailer. Rated as a 12 tonner, the Seddon had the Perkins 6.354 engine.

Built by Atkinson specifically to Adams requirements, MLT 329D incorporated a Cummins NH250B engine which drove through an Allison Torqmatic semi-automatic gearbox. Rated for up to 65 tons gross operation, the outfit also includes a rather special Dyson semi-trailer with a loading bed length which could be extended from 17'6" up to 26'. Although the 35 ton capacity dump truck from Blackwood Hodge was only loaded for demonstration purposes, an early job for regular driver Stan Ashby and this Atkinson special was taking a 34 ton section of transformer across to France.

Don Bewick was to follow in his father Martin's footsteps when he set up in haulage during 1946 with a brand new petrol engined Commer - FRM 315. He was to expand buying an ERF - HKB 239 - in 1947 and later a Leyland Cub which was ex BRS. Originally hauling livestock, Don moved onto flat work and was to sub contract a lot of traffic through BRS Whitehaven. 21 MRM dates from January 1963, the 12C/3AR model - chassis number L13242 - being regularly driven by Hughie Rickerby who worked for Bewicks for about five years. Pictured about to leave Workington, the Leyland Comet has about eight tons on it's back as it heads for Tilbury docks. Although Don retired from the haulage game about 1988, he still lives at Plumbland in north west Cumbria.

Born in 1925, Alfred Geoffrey Bird began his transport life during 1947 after doing service with the RAF. Geoff's first vehicle was an ex WD American Dodge which worked with Midland Tar Distillers, a customer which he was still serving 25 years later. However, it was to be in the field of heavy haulage where Birds created an impact although this 14' diameter storage tank was a fairly routine piece of work. The 150 Gardner powered ERF dates from 1961 and is coupled to a 45 ton capacity Crane 4 in line low loader.

Like most hauliers of the day, Geoff Bird's expansion was tightly controlled by the number of carriers licences he could lay his hands on. When Wright Bros of Crown Street, Wolverhampton were looking to sell off their heavy haulage vehicles to concentrate on crane business, Birds quickly snapped up the two Fodens, six Scammells and assortment of trailers. As the 1949 registration on this ex Wrights DG Foden outfit suggests, the 6x4 tractor had started it's civillian life with Sunters of Northallerton. The semi-trailer had originally been an American made 50' tandem axle flat, but Bird's engineer Ted Yardley made it far more practical by converting it to a step frame four axle 48 footer. The extra running gear being provided by Kirkstall made axles.

His mother's house in Hilton Lane at Shareshill had been Geoff Bird's first operating centre - just down the road from Alice Adams' cottage - but about 1958 he moved the half mile to these premises on the A460 at Featherstone. David Yardley is the mate supervising the reverse of 9449 VT, the 150 Gardner powered 1964 ERF being coupled to a Bird converted four axle semi-trailer. All up weight of this 60' long crane girder load was around the 40 ton mark. Geoff Bird was to live in the bungalow to the right of the office block and whilst this house has been demolished to make way for a BP filling station, the old Bird offices are now in use by the GCM concern.

Although BMCs were favoured for the long running Midland Tar Distillers work, Birds quickly adopted ERF as their heavyweight workhorse. New ERFs were usually supplied through the Beech dealership at Stoke-on-Trent. Ted Yardley recalls there was no shortage of volunteers when a new tractor had to be collected as Norman Beech

normally gave the driver a £10 note as a way of wishing the new unit well. Pictured heading southbound from the M6 services at Knutsford, Billy Stevens is at the wheel of his 1964 registered 1631 EH. The 70' long column he's carrying is enroute from Widnes Foundry to the West Midlands.

Whilst modular built six axle semi-trailers may be a regular sight in the 1990s, thirty years earlier they just didn't exist - apart from this Birds special. Engineer Yardley said this load carrier was very much a one off and built specifically to support the 55 ton pressure vessel it's pictured carrying. Being 70' long and 12' diameter, the load required the large number of axles to support the weight but more importantly to give enough travelling stability. Coming up with ideas like this didn't endear Birds to people like Wynns and Pickfords who would have transported such a vessel on two bogies hauled by a more expensive ballasted tractor. The Kirkstall running gear used here had an inbuilt freeplay of about 1" which allowed some tolerance to the tyre wear of a trailer which was otherwise unsteerable.

A driver's strike was to hit Birds about 1974 but the closure of the company occurred after Geoff Bird died of cancer at the age of 49. The assets were sold off although TBF 706D had gone prior to this sale. Vic Saunders is at the wheel of the ERF and whilst yard trailer man Des Hodgkins regularly rode at Vic's side, he wasn't one of the two mates in the cab. In a total of 489 lots, eleven ERF tractor units were brought under the hammer they being: ORF 949F, YEH 160H, OVT 915F, PVT 251F, PVT 252F, LEH 920E. MEH 267E, MVT 119E, YEH 161H, TVT 102G, KVT 814E. PHN 82F was a Guy Big J eight wheeler and JYC 253D a similarly configured Foden flat. MNA 767G was a Hydrocon Talisman 10 ton crane, whilst ERF 986 and 987K were a pair of rather rare S60 Foden 6x2 tractor units.

Opposite: This girder trailer was another Bird special built by Ted Yardley which sported an automatic steering system. A pair of JCB rams were incorporated into the neck and these were linked by hydraulic piping to the rear bogie. When the AEC turned, the movement was sensed in the rams and they in turn hydraulically operated the steering on the rear bogie. Bill Merrick was the driver of OBF 144D, the 40' long vessel being made by Forsters of Tipton. This Mammoth Major was rated for 56 tons gross operation but wasn't in service when the Bird fleet was auctioned off in 1974.

Bannered as the largest lorry in Britain used exclusively for transporting footwear by road, Bata put a Dodge outfit into service during July 1946. Fred Shelley collected the new artic from Carrimores of Finchley - who built the trailer and bodywork - although Albert Richards and driver's mate Lawrence Brown were it's normal crew. At 33' long and 12'6" high, the Dodge could carry 10,000 pairs of ordinary shoes or 20,000 pairs of plimsolls. The planning for the artic was to run north to Glasgow and then back load for Tilbury from the Bata factory at Maryport. CJN 980 was the second identical Dodge - with sleeping compartment above the normal cab - which like it's predecessor was found to be an ideal moving advert but down on power. The streamlined bodywork may have contributed to a fire which gutted one of the artics in South Wales. At their peak British Bata ran 21 vehicles on distribution work although currently contractors are used for this sort of delivery.

Due to their strategic importance - plus the fact that their purpose built garage offered covered accommodation for all the fleet - Nicholsons of Cockermouth were to see their business swallowed up by nationalisation. The coal round vehicles were sold separately but even though tippers were specifically exempted from the original Labour Government plans, 22 vehicles of Nicholsons were compulsorily taken. In practice there was little change for the driving staff or their working patterns as this line up of ex Nicholson vehicles sees them still working out of Threlkeld quarry - midway between Keswick and Penrith. Other Bedford tippers known to have passed into BRS ownership from Nicholsons were FAO 286, 287, 288 and 558 plus GAO 295, GRM 905 and HRM 176.

Ronnie Brown is pictured at the wheel of his ex Nicholson tipper, the Bedford supplied new through SMT of Carlisle in 1949. Being loaded by shovel at Threlkeld quarry with the mass of Skiddaw in the background, Ronnie only continued working out of Cockermouth for about two years. BRS were to close the old Nicholson depot and transfer the vehicles to Howgate at Whitehaven before eventually easing out of tipper work altogether. William Nicholson's son John - the other brothers being William and Robert - became a maintenance supervisor with BRS' Carlisle region although in 1954 he bought two old Austins and a Bedford to go back into haulage. Forty years on, John's son Peter still trades under the W S Nicholson title with three Scania artic tippers being operated out of Lorton Road, Cockermouth. Another grandson Eric Nicholson, also favours Scanias for his Cockermouth based operation.

The programme of nationalisation saw all manner of vehicles taken into Government ownership and although some remained to do the job they performed before being painted BRS red, many others were moved to different parts of the country. JE 5301 was new in 1939 to Almond Motors of Whaplode near Spalding and one of two similar four wheelers which were transferred to the old Reliance depot at Terrington St Clement, which was part of the Wisbech Group. Pictured on the A66 near Brough in 1950, the driver and photographer is the ex Reliance man Rowland Stanley Lane - or Jim as he was usually known. Loaded with empty fruit trays, the Gardner 4LK powered vehicle is returning from a trip to Glasgow - at a top speed of 32mph - having delivered strawberries to a jam factory up there.

Opposite: For five months of the year, these AEC Mammoth Majors must have been some of the hardest working vehicles in the entire BRS organisation. Because Bury St Edmunds' British Sugar Corporation factory only produced raw sugar, it was the task of these 12 bulkers to haul the unrefined mass to the Tate & Lyle premises at Silvertown. Working the sugar beet season between September and January, 24 hours a day, 7 days a week, doing two round trips per day - speed limit being 20mph - it didn't help the vehicles cause that BRS employed all manner of casual drivers to keep the wheels turning. Registered MPW 694-705, the AECs had consecutive chassis numbers 3871H829-840 when new into service in 1951. They were eventually replaced by a similar number of Bristol eight wheelers and because they were painted in BSC's blue livery - rather than the BRS red - were known as the Bury Blues.

Above: Before being allocated to Terrington St Clement from the Grimsby Group, this petrol engined ex WD Bedford had a fresh coat of paint and a new body fitted. Jim Lane is again the driver and he's pictured around 1950 in Victoria Street, Rugby. Heading for Robertsons Jam factory at Draylsden, Manchester, there's about six tons of strawberry pulp inside the barrels he's carrying. Whilst the fate of this Bedford isn't known, Jim was to spend the last 28 years of his driving career with Silver Roadways working on contract to British Sugar Corporation.

Above and below: As well as compulsory purchase of all manner of vehicles, the creation of BRS also meant a wide variety of depots were acquired, none more interesting perhaps, than the one at Abington. Situated on the A74 about 40 miles south of Glasgow, Neil Black was responsible for the original construction. Built in 1938, Exhibition Garage took it's name from the Empire Exhibition held at Glasgow during this year. The premises were to pass to Youngs Express before it was nationalised. As well as an operations base, BRS were also expected to keep up the business of selling fuel to the general public from the roundabout filling station. The depot must have been special as it employed it's own gardener while cattle transportation obviously was a major traffic both in and out of the area. The CX3 Albion seen collecting a box is in the colours of White Line Transport Co of Grangemouth. After being bought by Road Services (Caledonian), the depot was to pass to Sandy Reive who currently runs an ERF based fleet under the name of Reive & Grossart - although he no longer employs a gardener.

Tom Brown - christened Thomas Henry - went into road transport on May 9, 1932. At first in partnership with his brother William, he traded in his motor cycle to Lincolnshire Motors as part exchange for their first vehicle. Brought up in the Wolds village of Burgh on Bain, he moved the 20 miles to Waltham just outside Grimsby. After buying out his brother's interests, expansion was only modest although DFU 588 came brand new in 1947 and was one of two Foden four wheelers - the other being the '39 vintage BBE 908. Driver of DFU was George Cheffings - only the second man to be employed as a driver by Tom - and he normally ran between Brigg and Grimsby on sugar traffic. Although Browns weren't nationalised, the four strong fleet - a Leyland Comet and a Vulcan making up the quartet - were limited to working within a 25 mile radius of Waltham Post Office.

With tight controls in the heady days of nationalisation, Browns were only able to expand through Contract licences which meant you could only carry goods for one specified customer. GNR 988 and GUT 192 were two ERFs - bought through Newark Road garage from Parrs of Leicester - worked in 1951 on the Fison contract although MFW 245 came in 1955 for this traffic and was regularly driven by Charlie Webster. Together with sister Leyland Octopus NFU 131 - usually driven by Jack Martin - the eight wheelers did three trips a week from Fisons Immingham plant down to Avonmouth. The greedy boards on top of the body were to accommodate the back loads of coal from Rossington colliery near Doncaster, back to the Fisons plant. The 600 engine driving through a five speed direct top gearbox only produced a top speed of 35mph. It's recalled there was a plate inside the Leyland cab which read, 'Do not coast in neutral gear' but all Charlie Webster would say was, "I don't know of any other gear to coast in".

Tom Brown had a foreward outlook on haulage and in 1955 went into articulation with these two AEC Mercurys - MBE 822 and 823. Coupled to single axle Taskers semi-trailers, these very light outfits were usually driven by Jimmy Dixon and Don Chapman. As soon as allowed, Browns were buying carriers licences, although part of a strange job lot bought from BRS about 1954 was the old Winterton chapel which had been a Scunthorpe area repair depot. Pictured at Immingham docks, the Mercury's bagged traffic was sourced either through Fisons or British Titan Products.

Opposite: Although Browns ran a mixture of Leyland, AEC and Albion, most of these new vehicles were bought through the John Hudson dealership at Bawtry. PBE 20 came new in 1957, the Chieftan being one of three similar four wheelers fitted with Pilot tipping gear - the others being LBE 709 and 797. PBE was regularly driven by Mick Wilson who joined Browns in 1951 and stayed with the company until he retired in 1977. Mick was also on the Fisons contract taking bulk fertiliser to Goole then back loading with coal from Rossington. By 1958 the expanding Brown fleet had completely outgrown the drive beside Tom's house in Waltham and the firm moved to premises at Garth Lane in Grimsby.

Tom Brown was to expand in the early 1960s through buying up as many vehicles and licences he could afford. Three wagons - two Albions and a Commer - were bought from Cromwell Motors in Grimsby although their licences were soon transferred onto a Leyland Badger and two AEC Mercurys. A similar transfer deal took place when three vehicles of Hewsons were bought although the big bonus to this purchase was in how heavy the three vehicles were. Carriers licences stipulated the unladen weight of the respective vehicles they were issued to but as you were allowed to substitute weight for weight, Browns were able to double the number of vehicles being run on the old Hewson licences. In place of this 1934 Mark 1 AEC Mammoth Major - and two four wheeled AECs with drawbar trailers - Browns substituted a Leyland Badger and two Ford six wheelers fitted with insulated boxes plus three Albion four wheeled rigids. FW 5273 was the 13th eight wheeled chassis to be built by AEC and although new to Hewsons was perhaps better known for carrying a Bisto advert on it's side in it's earlier days.

Seen by Geoff Milne overnighting on Tyneside during 1969, LEE 21F was one of six brand new Scania Vabis tractors which Browns put into service. The first two - HEE 370E and 375E - were followed by LEE 20-23F with 21F normally driven by Dave Peart. The semi-trailer pictured belongs to Trailer Express who worked the TOR line between Immingham and Sweden. A big expansion of Brown's operation was overseen by traffic manager Jack Martin and by 1969 the 44 strong fleet had outgrown the Garth Lane premises. It was moved to their current HQ on Estate Road 1 although Browns interests in Scania were also to expand. Approached by the manufacturer to take over the local agency in 1967, the family owned firm still runs the Scanlink Grimsby dealership which is next door to the haulage and warehousing operations. Tom's son Martin now heads up the Brown fleet which is more than 50 strong.

Up until 1930, Charlie Burn had been a farm worker on the estate of Colonel Ernest Vaux at Brettenby Manor near Barton. But when the Colonel got sick of driving his beasts down to market, it was suggested to Charlie that he bought a wagon. Supplied by Sherwoods of Darlington, HN 7371 was a Chevrolet which started out on livestock and farm based work. Brother Peter got his first vehicle - a Dennis in 1931 - and then younger brother Paul had Bedford three tonner AHN 217 in October 1934.

Believed to be the first artic in the area, RH 6748 was bought second hand from the farmer Jack Metcalfe of Piercebridge about 1935. The partnership between the three brothers - Charles Patrick Mascot, Peter Vivian Morrison Baden and Paul Francis Ninian - was formalised under the Burn Bros title and their base at The Stenning in Barton is still the firm's HQ, 60 years on. Bought for it's extra carrying capacity, this Bedford-Carrimore outfit normally ran empty every day down to Hull to collect feed for the Darlington based merchant CM Varley. Capable of an amazing 10 ton payload, one extra fitted by the brothers was the oversize offside mirror. It was the rather zealous policeman who worked the road between York and Market Weighton which the brothers really had eyes for.

Peter Burn recalls the 1930s agricultural haulage rates were rather poor so encouraged to go on long distance work, they put into service CVK 355 in February 1936. Coupled to a Scammell semi-trailer, the Bedford was ran on sub contract to the clearing house of Ex Army Transport Ltd whose nearest office was in Newcastle. With an unladen weight of 3 ton 19cwt, the artic was limited to 20 mph although caught for doing 30mph on the only three lane stretch of the A1 - between Bawtry and Doncaster - Peter Burn was fined £6. It was money problems of another kind - the realisation that Ex Army were taking more than their 10% cut - which forced the brothers to find their own traffic, a lot of this being ICI wallboards destined for Scotland.

When their haulage business was in the balance, the Burn brothers decided to keep their options open by going into private hire. "We were sick of roping and sheeting," said Peter Burn but what wasn't anticipated was the mess which so many passengers could create and clearing out their bus every night could be quite a headache. With a price tag of £2,011, the 33 seater Duple bodied Bedford earned it's keep mainly during the summer months on day trips to Blackpool, the Lake District or down to the seaside. The brothers soon realised this wasn't their best idea and within two-three years, they'd sold the vehicle on - for £1,800 - to Scurrs of Stillington.

War time operations of Burn Bros were fairly low key although Bedfords which came into service during that period were FHN 561 in 1939, CKY 932 in 1941 and GHN 213 on February 2, 1942. More vehicles came in the late 1940s and by the time of nationalisation, Burns were asked to sell all 11 of their fleet into government ownership. Rather than agree, the brothers - assisted by accountant Bert Coates - decided to fight the decision by adopting every administrative delaying tactic in the book. They should have finally disappeared on March 22, 1951 but a change of government earned their reprieve. PHN 406 came on November 2, 1951 and given to Les Jolly, it had a top speed potential of 60mph. The last petrol engined Bedford into service, it didn't receive a Meadows diesel conversion unlike the similar S type OHN 695 - an artic unit which was new on April 2, 1951.

HVN 531 was Burns first eight wheeler which came new on July 3, 1952, with a price tag of £5,030. A similar Foden was JPY 106 - new on February 9, 1953 - although GKC 256 was a second hand Foden six wheeler which was bought on March 25, 1954. This was the day that a Dennis four wheeler - MUP 676 - which hauled an Eagle 6 ton drawbar trailer went into service. The brothers sole Foden S20 artic, RPY 268, was new on December 7, 1957, it proving to be one of their finest servants. Priced at £5,068 - split £3,561 for the tractor and £1,507 for the Taskers semi-trailer - it's spec' included a Mark II two stroke engine and 12 speed gearbox. Regular drivers were George Potter and Arthur Ash whose son Harry now drives at Burns. This S20 was operated until 1970 when it was written off after an accident in Stockton.

Burn Bros first office at Glasgow was in McAlpine Street and with regular traffic from ICI demanding next day delivery into Scotland, an overnight trunk service was established. Pictured loaded for 7pm departure are 72 APY - with Derek Ainsley and Johann Jankowski as it's regular drivers - and RVN 863 which normally had Ray Clark or Frank Johnson behind the wheel. At their peak, five vehicles a night were leaving Barton for their pre-arranged change over with five south bound scottish vehicles at the Moss Cafe, just north of Carlisle. Talk to residents of Penrith in the early '60s and they'll probably tell you how they could almost set their clocks as the Burn Bros Foden two strokes bellowed through the town centre narrows. RVN 863 was new into service on March 31, 1958, whilst 72 APY dates from 1961.

Robert Cawthorn and Keith Sinclair put their names to one of the north east's finest concerns which was to grace the transport scene for more than 30 years. Although their HQ was on Durham Road at Birtley, Cawthorns were to soon establish a chain of UK depots which were linked by intensive trunking operations. The company was one of the first in the region to run driver accompanied vehicles over the Channel and after establishing their first Continental office in Paris, they moved on to serve the whole of western Europe. JCN 965 isn't however believed to have crossed the water, the Gardner 6LX-150 powered eight wheeler model L1786XT coming new in 1959 and being normally driven by Archie Hewitt.

After the Foden two strokes, Burn Bros bought some Mark 5 AEC Mandators which transformed the night time operations. The AECs were the first vehicles capable of doing the 318 mile round trip to Motherwell and back without the need of a change over at the Moss. Volvo F86s were bought in the late 1960s, the others in the line being OVN 322G, UVN 675J and PAJ 844G, the Scania 110 being LHN 588K. The drivers in the photograph are - left to right - Tony Martin, Bobby Roberts and Ernie Garside. Pictured outside Shaw's foundry on Forty Foot road in Middlesbrough, their loads are specially designed Bruce Anchors intended for use in the oil rig business. Following a restructuring of Burn Bros in 1986, the firm passed into the ownership of Chip and Geoff Burn who are the respective sons of Charlie and Peter Burn. The cousins currently operate six assorted Scanias on general haulage out of the old Barton base.

Robert Cawthorn's involvement in road haulage went back to 1921. He was to become manager of Northumbrian Transport Services - which was later nationalised - and after six months with BRS, he took over a directorship with Cockburn & Gunn. Under Cawthorn's influence, Cockburn's involvement in transport evolved back into general haulage although in 1954 the company of Cawthorn & Sinclair was created. In 1955 the vehicles of the two concerns were combined and this rare photograph of the fleet mix at that time shows the predominance of Atkinson multi-wheelers. The figure on top of FCN 126 is Andy Robson - Cawthorn's long serving fleet engineer - whilst Jimmy Brewis ropes down. ECN 930 was normally driven by Jackie Howard, an ex Durham Chemicals driver. Ronnie 'Blondie' Clarkson is on the back of his FCN 218 whilst Sid Dunn normally drove ECN 512, which is fifth in line.

Above: By 1961 Cawthorns were running a fleet in excess of 40 strong. Buying brand new, Robert Cawthorn was able to link registration with fleet numbers. LCN 59 and 62 were similar to LCN 63 which sports the distinctive star surround of the fleet number which was to become a company hallmark. Norman Emery got this Atkinson new, the standard spec' being a 6LX engine, ZF six speed gearbox and single drive rear bogie. The Atkinsons were returning 12mpg carrying a 17 ton payload with night runs operated to Birmingham, London, South Wales, Manchester and Liverpool whilst Glasgow bound loads changed drivers at Gretna Green.

Opposite above: In 1962 Cawthorns were running three Atkinson eight wheeled tankers on black oil work. Usually ran between Jarrow and Cumberland or up to Blyth Power Station, the seasonal fluctuations of their traffic meant it was ideal for some of the older chassis'. However, coming new into service in 1962, OCN 68 was something entirely different. Ran on contract to Procter & Gamble, it was it's 195 bhp Rolls Royce B81 petrol engine which made it such a head turner. Quiet, smooth and very quick, one of it's drawbacks related to it's modest fuel consumption of only 4-5mpg. Reliability was another question mark with the concept vehicle and engineer Robson knew that when the ringing 'phone woke him at 4am, it was normally the ERF driver 'Seppy' telling him the petrol engine wouldn't start. The ERF went through four Rolls B81 engines - and numerous front brake discs - before a diesel turbo engined Pekins was fitted to see the tanker's life out.

Opposite below: The Thorn contract was a big reason behind Cawthorn's expansion and although this trio of TK Bedfords sport Enfield registrations, the distinctive fleet number clearly indicates the north east parentage. Pictured leaving the Pallion works at Sunderland, the vehicles are fully loaded with black & white television tubes. Cawthorns were to run a five day trunk service between Wearside and London with ten Bedfords running in each direction. There isn't a lot of weight being carried on the BTC 4 in line semi-trailers, thus the reason why the lightweight TKs were specified, but the speed and distance of the regular work took it's toll on the Bedford 330 engines. One garage on the A1 at Markham Moor near Newark made a lot of money by towing in these outfits when they'd expired at almost the mid point of their haul.

34

In 1963 Cawthorns switched their allegiance from Atkinson eight wheeled rigids to ERF artics for their maximum weight vehicles. Gardner remained the favoured engine option although Cummins 205s were taken when the former were not available. £4,715 was the 1965 price tag for CCN 286C which is pictured with Jack Stapleford at the wheel about to leave the Caterpillar factory at Birtley. Cawthorns operated a six day service for Caterpillar and created the depots at Ashby-de-la-Zouch and Uddington near Glasgow specifically to meet this customer's requirements. The large headboard on the Boden semi-trailer carrying a load of bined parts, indicates how a tilt body could be built up onto the trailer if so required.

Dennis Hutchings, the Transport Controller of Thorn-AEI, had more than 20,000 vehicles under his control and he oversaw the upgrading of Cawthorns TK based fleet to favour heavier weight Dodges. With Perkins 6.354 engine and Eaton two speed axle, these units were operated between 1967 and 1972 when Leyland Lynx tractor units were put onto this work. Magirus Deutz units were to follow in 1977. Full capacity tandem axle semi-trailers took the place of the 4 in lines so that if required, the load carriers could be used for other than TV tube work. On October 1, 1971, the Cawthorn Group passed into the ownership of Tozer, Kemsley and Millbourn (Holdings) Ltd for £1.1 million. At that time the fleet consisted of 180 tractor units plus 400 trailers and outlying depots were listed as Dundee, Glasgow, Skelmersdale, Birmingham, London, Port Talbot and Le Havre.

Opposite: About 1963 Cawthorns began running into France, their first driver accompanied traffic being television tubes. It wasn't long however before Procter & Gamble also had some of their specialised material taken over the Channel. It was an advertising pitch during the 1960s that the perfume involved in the manufacture of Camay soap cost a guinea an ounce. Long serving drivers like Norman Emery - who drove ECN 389D - would tell you that a drawback of hauling this traffic was that your cab smelt like a lady's boudoir.

Below left: As the road fleet expanded, so did the company's general interests. Cawthorns established the concern of Birtley Car & Commercials not only to build, paint and repair the fleet's vehicles - plus other people's as well - but also to establish a car and commercial dealership. Due to an inability to get sufficient numbers of ERF tractor units for their own purposes - never mind other prospective purchases - the dealership took the Mercedes agency so obviously the Cawthorn fleet began to favour this marque. Long serving driver Keith Turner is pictured beside his LPS 1418, the Boden semi-trailer supporting a load of Caterpillar pieces for export. Strangely Cawthorns didn't go totally over to Mercedes as the late 1960s saw the arrival of the first of many Volvos.

Below: Cawthorns soon identified that early European traffic was being hampered by the small number of permits which were being made available to them. One way round this restriction was to set up an office in Paris and as early as 1965, the company had four ERFs registered and based in France. By 1972 this figure had grown to 16, an indicator of the booming expansion to Cawthorn's international work. The 1970s saw the company firmly established but the recession of the early '80s hit them hard as major customers declined. In September 1983 the TKM subsidiary of Cave Wood took management responsibility of Cawthorns but in August 1984 the Birtley depot was closed. One branch of Cawthorns which was to remain in the north east was Birtley Car & Commercials. In 1994, it's direct descendants are still occupying the old Cawthorn premises. John English and ex Cawthorn man Bill Mustard trade under the name of English Mustard offering services to the car and commercial world.

When Winchester based Alf Neale retired on June 26, 1960, his diploma stated he had clocked up 44 years of service with the railways. The majority of the time had been with Chaplins who specialised in distribution from the rail network. 'Nellie' as he was known, recalls he spent most of his days delivering pacels to the upstarts of Winchester college. Seen about 1931 in Greenhill Road, Winchester, his daughters Phyllis and Gwen are in the cab of his A series Ford. Chaplins were to be taken over by Pickfords although on nationalisation, the Winchester based vehicles passed into Southern Railways custody.

Opposite: About 1921 Alan went into haulage in partnership with his mother Josephine Mary. Three American built FWD wagon and trailer combinations were operated primarily on long timber work although this photograph taken at Alnwick sees a load of fabricated steelwork on board which is believed to be intended for colliery headgear equipment. Re-engined with four cylinder petrol Dormans, the permanent four wheel drive vehicle was capable of about 16mph. With constantly working in the mills, the effect of sawdust in his lungs caused Alan's death in 1928. His brother Geoffrey returned from Australia but rather than retain the haulage business, he turned to agricultural engineering and pipe laying, a trade currently continued by his son Leslie from North Togston near Amble.

Above: A cabinet maker by trade, Alan Christian's life was one of continual involvement with wood. Based on the A1 road at Newton on the Moor - just south of Alnwick - Alan devised this sophisticated timber extraction outfit in 1906. These were the days when teams of horses or traction engines normally dragged trees out using sheer brute strength. His locomotive started life as a motor car built by the French manufacturer Panhard & Le Vassor. Once worn out for road use, Alan received extended life from it running on this narrow gauge railway.

When TN 543 started life as a conventional six wheeler carrying Bero flour, I suppose it never imagined it would end it's days in this guise. Thomas Cook bought the petrol engined Thornycroft six wheeler hoping it would give him even better off road traction. Diff locks were still to be invented however so he tried to improve matters by only having twin tyres on the first driving axle but ran the tyres at different pressures to cut down on heat generation. It still never ran very well although Thomas was able to buy a brand new diff from the army sales for only half a crown (12.5p). Pictured in the grounds of Castle Howard, the figures include Septimus Cook - the driver - and his mate Harry Robinson sitting at the rear of the Welatonian tree whilst it's new owner, Mr Whittaker of Malton, has his hand on it.

Thomas Cook was to have three daughters - Barbara, Bella and Betsy - plus four sons - Siddle, Martin, Jimmy and Seppy - all of whom were to have some involvement in the family transport business. Jimmy Cook was always said to be the smallest so he was given this small Bedford to drive. No concession however was made in the size of his loads and he's pictured about to leave Hutton Gate near Guisborough which in 1938 was still in North Yorkshire. 'The Wanderer' was hardly a few months old, it being ran on contract to J W Tunnicliffe of Silsden. With Jimmy is the second man Thomas Bartrop, who was actually Jimmy's nephew as he was the son of Bella Cook and her husband Jim Bartrop.

Below: Seventh in the Cook family was the aptly named Septimus. Once Thomas Cook had died in 1942, the business was split up and although his brother Siddle expanded steadily, Seppy preferred an owner driver's life. Of all the vehicles he ran 'Lady Mary' gave him the most reliable service and it was to clock up almost 2 million miles. The 1938 model was actually refurbished and re-registered in 1955. Seppy's pictured with one of the many Stewart & Lloyd loads of 50' long gas pipes which he hauled from Coatbridge to Winchester and Southampton on behalf of the Southern Gas Board. After selling up his vehicles in 1968 to Stillers of Darlington, Seppy and his wife Mary were to establish a clearing house business in Darlington. Although he's since died, S & M C Transport is still active in this line of work.

The family owned Cross concern grew to be one of the most respected names in the Wolverhampton sand & gravel business. John Cross had been the blacksmith in the Staffordshire village of Gailey - where the A5 crosses the A449 - but it was when he moved into premises on Willenhall Road in Wolverhampton that the business really flourished. Photographer A B Hart recorded this premium line up featuring Leyland, Daimler and Ford load carriers during October 1931. Two of the figures recognised are brothers Harry Cross - on the extreme right - and Arthur Cross, seen third from right and as the dust coat indicates, was usually in charge of the garage. The other Cross sons were George and Jack, the family business offering tyre repairs as well as transport - including a contract for the delivery of Banks' beer - plus sand, gravel and granite supply. The former activity is rather apt as in 1994 the old Cross premises were being occupied by an outlet of Central Tyres.

By 1961 the Cross business was still being operated out of the same premises but as these Robert Bate photographs illustrate, Fords had become the sole Cross workhorse. The vehicles worked out of two main quarries, one near Penkridge, the other near Wombourne. Whilst all the early '50s Ford Thames 'Costcutters' and some of the later Traders are painted in the old navy blue livery, the latest Thames Traders feature the changed canary yellow and black colours. All the Cross vehicles were bought new from either Don Everall or B Billingham, the two Wolverhampton Ford dealerships. The Cross business ended about 1967 when the two last surviving brothers decided to sell out to the Redland Group.

In six years, Derek Freeland had grown from a sole second hand Commer TS3 artic to this impressive line up - all bought second hand. Pictured around 1978 in the Greenbank Road depot, Aberdeen, Freeland Freight had rode the oil boom which hit the granite city in the '70s. Most of the fleet were operated on local time work - a new concept for platform artics - although Freelands sole long distance vehicle was the Dodge 16 ton gross rigid - third from the right - driven by Dod Allan. ERG 563D and EFU 371L were the company's first two bonneted Mercedes LS1418s - pictured on the left. The marque is still favoured in the 1994 fleet which is now more than 40 strong. Derek recalls that he adopted his yellow livery in 1972 after being impressed by a Ford Escort Mexico saloon car of the same colour which his cousin had just bought.

In 1932, at the age of 24, Leonard Green was running a Reo four wheeler on a coal round in Parkgate, Rotherham. Although the railways had the monopoly of all the local steel traffic, Leonard was asked to do the odd load and the association with Parkgate Iron & Steel Co was formed. During the late 1940s when his fleet was nationalised, Leonard went into the taxi business, made generators for the fairground people and even manufactured pop corn which he sold to the local cinemas. MVT 670 dates from 1948 and was the sixth vehicle in the post de-nationalisation fleet. 'Big Alf' Leadbetter is the long serving Green driver in this Frank Cuckson photograph and Alf well recalls going to North Wales with Leonard to buy fleet number 7 - CUN 89. The ERF four wheeler cost £500 and as Leonard received so much cash from his Showmen customers to pay for the generators, he paid for this vehicle in 6d (2.5p) pieces.

In 1947 Greens were running a fleet of 40 strong but rather than see all his vehicles compulsorily acquired by BRS, 20 were sold to Parkgate Iron & Steel to form the basis of their fleet. Leonard's younger brother Frank went with these vehicles to become Parkgate's transport manager. By 1953 Leonard was firmly back on the haulage scene and this line up was pictured to mark the opening of the 11 inch continuous bar mill at Parkgate. The two ERF eight wheelers are Parkgate's 20 & 21 driven by Tommy Morris and George Welsh. JTW 740 was the Gardner 5LW powered ERF driven by Percy Reeder and Jimmy Welsh, it's hauling one of the three Taskers trombone trailers ran by Greens. Ahead of the ERFs is Parkgate's internal fire appliance, one of three similar Lister powered units - the other two being a dumper and a flat.

Parkgate operated two Scammell box tractors between 1953 and 1963, MWR 152 being sister to fleet number 50. Norman Graham worked 12 hour shifts on MWR 171 with his relief being another 12 hour man, Luke Prendergast. Although mainly used on internal work, one of the Scammells was taxed so that it could run the two miles down the public roads to the Roundwood bar mill. Nominally rated as 25 tonners, Norman recalls the little Scammells regularly moved loads of 52 tons, inside the works. A mate was only carried if the Scammell went off site so Norman became expert in being able to hook up to any of the seven Dyson drawbar trailers single handed.

Even when they lost their fleet to BRS, Greens still serviced the vehicles of Parkgate Iron & Steel Co. Under Green's influence, Parkgate continued to buy ERFs including a batch of six 'Sabrina' six wheeled tippers, all but one of which were powered by the Gardner 6LW engine. Nicknamed after a famous model of the late 1950s because of their curved lines, 35 was regularly driven by Granville Thorpe. The biggest incident in this ERF's life was when it hit an overhead tree - Granville wasn't driving - whilst the body was raised and it completely sheared the body from the chassis, although it was later repaired Normally ran between Parkgate furnace bay and the tip at Ravenfield, these six scow ended tippers are not to be confused with the two Sabrina dumpers - 100 & 102 - which ran internally at up to 50 tons gross.

Leonard Green was to buy his first ERF - an eight wheeler - in 1936. The vehicle had been a motor show exhibit which had originally been ordered by a brewery, but when the order was cancelled, Green established a relationship with the marque which was to last more than 30 years. All his ERFs had to be Gardner powered and some ex BRS four wheelers which came with the AEC 7.7 litre engine had them replaced with 4LK/LWs before going into service. About 20 of Greens four wheelers were used on the GEC contract which saw them haul washing machines & cookers nationwide from the nearby Swinton factory. To service GEC Birmingham, Greens based five vehicles in the midlands, this arrangement being formalised when the goodwill of A Mason from Smethwick was bought and their old premises rented. One famous GEC non ERF missing from this line up is JMA 30, the ex Jowetts of Rowmarsh Foden coach which was stripped then rebodied as a van by Jennings. In this line up NWY 716 has been saved for preservation by Harold Fillingham of Bramley.

Parkgate's most powerful Sabrinas were their half dozen ballast box tractors which were bought to service the newly created Aldwark site in 1963. Although they were registered, they were exempted from road tax as they did less than six miles per week on the public roads. A Rolls Royce 200bhp engine drove a three speed gearbox via a torque converter to produce a phenomenal vehicle. Running up to 220 tons gross, it's not surprising these ERFs could go through a set of tyres in two months. Whilst Norman Graham drove fleet number 108, Lol Kemp and mate Andy Tummons are pictured in 107 - 577 EWT. The wooden prop which chocked the small bonnet open was a standard mod' because of the excessive heat generated by these vehicles' transmissions when working under load.

Pictured tipping into a hopper at the slag reduction plant on August 11, 1964, Don Watson is the figure behind the wheel of the distinctive fleet number 42. It wasn't just the twin headlights which differentiated this Sabrina from the others, in the main it was it's smooth and powerful Gardner 6LX-150 engine. Don began his driving at Parkgate on the external fleet before moving onto internal operations and up the driving tree to finish on the big tractors before his retirement in 1993. 917 GWX ended it's days prematurely in 1970. Another driver inadvertently drove off with the body raised and the collision with a 13' high bridge snapped the ERF chassis in two.

In 1961, at the age of 53, Leonard Green died in hospital following a heart attack. At this time nearly 80 vehicles were in service with almost half of these being based at Smethwick. Keeping the business going fell to his sons - Leonard junior & Colin - and his two daughters Eileen & Kathleen. After taking on an ERF agency about 1964, Greens became Dennis agents with WWT 383G being one of three similar Maxim artic units which they put into service. Perkins V8 powered fleet number 1 was driven by Pete Kitchen although fleet number 4 - TWY 813F - came from the Kelvin Hall Motor Show complete with chromed wheel nuts and was given to 21 year old Alan Graham. Although Greens continued to operate, long term problems over Leonard senior's estate forced it's closure in 1977.

XSP 460 was Guard Bridge's fifth Octopus and in 1963 they took delivery of this pair of Power Plus 680 powered eight wheelers. Archie Barnett normally drove 4802 FG and if ever a vehicle was to leave it's mark as a solid workhorse, then this was the one. After doing first line service for 10 years, it was converted into the company's recovery vehicle and ran on trade plates 141 FG. After being damaged itself in a minor accident, it had the front of a Scammell Crusader transplanted to convert it into a six wheeler - and it's still in service. Alec McNaughton from the traffic office is the figure in 2130 FG although the vehicle was normally driven by Alec Cram who is recalled for his dead pan sense of humour.

Paper has been produced at Guard Bridge in Fife for more than 100 years. Historically the company had always relied on ships and then the rail network to deliver their highest quality writing and printing paper. In 1956 deliveries of paper were halted because of a rail strike and the then Managing Director - GP Adam - said never again would the company be forced into a position where they couldn't distribute their own products. In that year this quartet of 680 engined Leyland Octopus' was delivered from Joseph Wilkinsons of Edinburgh. At first the dealer took care of any major repairs but the drivers Alec Cram, Archie Barnett, Arthur Meldrum and Andrew Smith did their own oil changes and greasing. The distinctive dark blue and grey liveried eight wheelers tramped all over the UK although back in Guard Bridge they were known as BEFs - back every Friday.

Guard Bridge never ran a fleet number 13 instead 12A was the company's only Atkinson artic - DFG 75C. Not surprisingly some dyed in the wool Leyland drivers wouldn't touch the Atky as they felt the only good place for it's Gardner engine was in the back of a boat. KSP 137 and 138G plus LFG 691G were three Leyland Beavers fitted with semi-automatic gearboxes which came into service during October 1968. Whilst drivers Ian Black and Dave Pryde - both still with the company - had the occasional loss of gear, in fitter Bill Brown, Guard Bridge had someone who could work miracles with these 'boxes.In May 1972, TSP 54K, the company's first Scammell Handyman was taken into service. In 1973 a restructuring saw the transport fleet moved into a separate entity and trade under the name of Scotflow Ltd. The current blue and white livery was adopted in 1982, the year when ERF began to replace Leyland as favoured traction. The company, which is now part of James River Fine Papers Ltd, currently runs 24 vehicles.

Christopher 'Kit' Herring, having previously managed his father Jack's similar business, set up on his own account as a rag, bone, iron and steel merchant in the mid 1930s. Kit's first yard was in Baltic Street, West Hartlepool and his first vehicle was a four wheeled rulley, pulled by a single horse power. It wasn't long before motorised load carriers were being bought with Bedford and Thornycroft four wheelers ran before their first ERF 44G arriving in 1958. The Herring business had eventually evolved into providing road haulage for the people from whom they'd first collected scrap metal. Dick Mitchell - who later moved into the traffic office - was one of Herring's early long serving drivers, loads from the Expanded Metal Company taking him and the ERF all over the country.

JEF 367 was Herring's first ERF eight wheeler and it's recalled it came in 1960 with a price tag of £2,000. By then, Chris Herring junior had come into the family business which had adopted limited status. Although the Baltic Street yard was retained for some time, Kit Herring had diversified and he set up a garage in the town's Stockton Road. Selling under the banner of 'Good Class Cars', Kit also ran his wagons from the rear of the premises until an office was built on their large site at Longhill. Bob Cairns is pictured just outside the depot with a full 16 ton of Expanded Metal on the back of his 68GX.

Herring's first artics were Bedford powered and painted blue in the contract colours of Reeds Corrugated Cases. Whilst Albions were bought strongly as four wheeled rigids, ERF remained the heavyweight traction favourite coupled to Boden semi-trailers to handle full loads of South Durham steel. Herrings had expanded into general haulage through buying up the licences of a number of local concerns including Ogle Bros, Thomas Hauxfield, Arnold & Hildreth and Shaw's Scrap Metal. Processing scrap still continues to be a big part of the Herring business which is now run by Chris junior since his father died in 1987. The company's fleet size is around the 30 mark although the local operating skip carriers have more than 350 skips to move round. Seddon Atkinson has been strongly favoured since the first Borderers were taken into service about 1969.

Cousins and partners Charles and Steve Hoggarth currently run a 14 strong Volvo based fleet on a mix of milk and general haulage. The company bears the name of their grandfather Atkinson who in 1928 was the Glaisdale blacksmith. Deciding that horse hauled transport was on the way out and he would soon be out of a job, he went first into livestock haulage and then into churn transport after the Milk Marketing Board was formed in 1933. His sons Reg - in the picture - William and Frank came into the business but after only getting 2mpg from some petrol engined GMCs and Dodges, the brothers bought six Albion Chieftans. Sporting much travelled Michelin tyres, PVK 865 dates from 1952. The specially designed Sherwood bodied vehicle was usually driven by Miles Cook whose normal delivery point was Cox's Dairy in Whitby. In 1975 Hoggarths moved to their current base at Selly Hill - two miles out of Whitby. This ex Army ordnance depot had been the base of Aceys Transport before it was bought by the Slater Group prior to being sold to Hoggarths.

Opposite: Pictured at Earles Court in 1958, HEG 703 had actually arrived at the Motor Show badged as an AEC. However, when it was realised there weren't sufficient Maudslay vehicles on show, a swift alteration to this vehicle's badge was called for. In service the Mercury complete with leather bonnet covers became the pride and joy of Sam Rudd, who like Les Kirman was an ex Reliance Transport driver. The tartan interior to the Homalloy cab was rather fitting as Sam's normal load of 26 drops usually took him north of the border. Once he'd delivered all his tinned produce, a visit to the Cerbos factory at Greatham in County Durham usually produced a back load of salt. In 1968 the identity of Lin Can was lost when the company was taken over by Del Monte.

Above: Up until nationalisation, Lincolnshire Canners had always relied on small outside haulage contractors to deliver their produce. But, when British Road Services came onto the scene, Lin Can felt the multi drop method of distribution which they required couldn't be provided by the newly created government concern. With their head office at Boston, Lin Can's first fleet in 1950 was a massive investment in more than 20 Seddon four wheelers - some of the registrations being CJL 631, 634, 951, 953, DDO 483 and EDO 341. First painted blue, transport manager Bill Lewis was to oversee the fleet colour change to white. LEG 40 dates from 1960, the Seddon pictured at West Lynn with Les Kirman at the wheel. Les joined Lin Can in 1952 and his usual pattern of work saw him travel up to central London with close to 48 drops on his back.

Based at Wallacehill garage in Kilmarnock, the fleet of McCall & Greenshields are recalled for their striking racing green livery adorned with tartan and individual vehicle names. The company was founded by Alex 'Sandy' McCall and John Greenshields who in 1922 were a milkman and butcher respectively. John Greenshields died in the late 1920s but when Sandy bought his share, he also retained the original trading name to differentiate himself from nephew John McCall, another Kilmarnock haulier. JCS 916 was rated as a six tonner, the Perkins engined Seddon coming new on July 11, 1956. The broad and strong John Glover was this vehicle's regular driver, it's load being a set of Glenfield sluice gates.

Opposite: Sandy McCall was able to prevent his fleet from being nationalised by a combination of hauling exempted traffic - milk churns - and respecifying his remaining vehicles on contract licences. Pictured in 1954, his line up does not include a Commer four wheeler SX 7537 which was bought during December '54 specifically for it's Special A carriers licence. Within four weeks the Commer was part exchanged, whilst transferring the licence to GCS 819, a new Atkinson eight wheeler with chassis number FC 3508 and a total price tag of £2,258. Quickest vehicle on show here was 'Dodger' Rowlands Albion Chieftan churn carrier FCS 743. Hurrying to beat John Maitland to the dairy to unload his milk first one day, the high speed diff allowed him to reach 42mph. Joe Frew and John McLarty drove two other churn wagons whilst Bobby Burnie drove CSD 512.

Below: M&G's first vehicle was a Leyland - GB 967 - which was known as the battle axe because it's previous owner used to deliver Battle Axe sweets with it. Three chain drive solid tyred Albions were to follow and the Scottish made marque soon became a favourite. CS 7920 came new on May 21, 1938, the Albion eight wheeler having a Gardner 6LW engine. 'Wallacehill Majestic' was probably McCalls greatest servant as it stayed for 24 years. Pictured in Glenfields premises, Bob Young was it's first driver although David Rowland was driving when it worked the milk bottle night shift. This job saw loads of crated milk distributed on behalf of Scottish CWS to Ayr, Prestwick, Tarbolton and Annbank for the various schools in the area. Other Albions listed in the 1949 fleet list were CS 5149, CS 6658, CS 1499, CS 3039 and AAG 916. Also listed then were a Leyland CS 5418 and a Morris CS 6634.

Above: With a fleet mix of lightweight four wheelers and heavyweight eight wheelers, Sandy McCall adopted limited status in 1957. OCS 427 was new on January 1, 1960, it joining similar Austin 7 tonners HSD 36 - 1.11.55 - and KAG 919 which was first registered on March 26, 1957. OSD 374 came on March 25, 1960 and the fourth Austin RSD 929 went into service on May 1, 1961. All these general haulage four wheelers weighed unladen around the 3ton 11cwt mark.

Opposite above: Glenfield & Kennedy's engineering premises grew to cover about 150 acres in Kilmarnock. With McCalls responsible for most of their traffic, these 10 ton 16' high water strainers were a regular load destined for all parts of the world. GSD 27 was new into service on January 31, 1955, the 6LW powered eight wheeler tipping the scales unladen at 7ton 13cwt 3qrs. 'Roadster' ran on Contract licence for Glenfields whilst LAG 740 had an Open 'A' licence which meant it could carry goods for anyone, anywhere. 'Magnet' weighed off at 7ton 19cwt when new into service on January 4, 1958. McCalls bought their Atkinsons through John Mitchell of Greenock.

Opposite below: PCS 412 was to be McCalls only Foden, the Gardner 6LX powered eight wheeler tipping the scales at 7ton 16cwt when coming new into service on June 28, 1960. It operated with an Open 'A' licence although it's pictured at Wallacehill carrying a 14ton Glenfield valve. Dave McCulloch was regular driver of 'Major' which was to end it's days at McCalls when sold to Sam Andersons of Newhouse.

Opposite: VRG 804 was a rare second hand Atkinson purchase at McCalls, the outfit being pictured in the Glenfield works loading a hefty sluice gate with Jimmy McQuillan at the wheel. SSD 459 was to be Sandy's last new purchase. December 5, 1961, saw the Atkinson eight wheeler on the road but within three weeks it's owner had died. Gangrene had forced the amputation of Sandy's legs and his last few years were spent in a wheelchair. Jessie Roxburgh - whose long service had earned her a directorship - ran the company until it was sold as a going concern in 1963 to Bill Borland. McCalls then became a subsidiary of James Borland & Sons Ltd, a company which had been a Kilmarnock feed merchant since 1750.

Above: With Chic Rolphe taking over the day to day running, it was business as usual at McCalls. Bill Borland however did wish to change the name of McCalls to Cargo Express but he was prevented in doing so by Companies House for almost 20 years. Making do with the slogan on the side or front of his vehicles, these included eight semi-trailer vans used on nylon traffic out of Chemstrand. The 30' long vans - which were later stretched to 40 footers - had an internal system of floor mounted rails and rollers which allowed pallets to be loaded quickly. Sister to 229D - 'Wallacehill Concorde' - this Guy Invincible was usually driven by Andrew Boon on distance work but shunted locally by Gordon Beveridge. One of the last new vehicles to be painted green, a white colour scheme was used from1969. The name of Cargo Express Ltd was adopted in 1980 and Bill Borland's son Kenny currently runs a six strong fleet of vans under this title out of premises on Kilmarnock's Moorfield Industrial Estate.

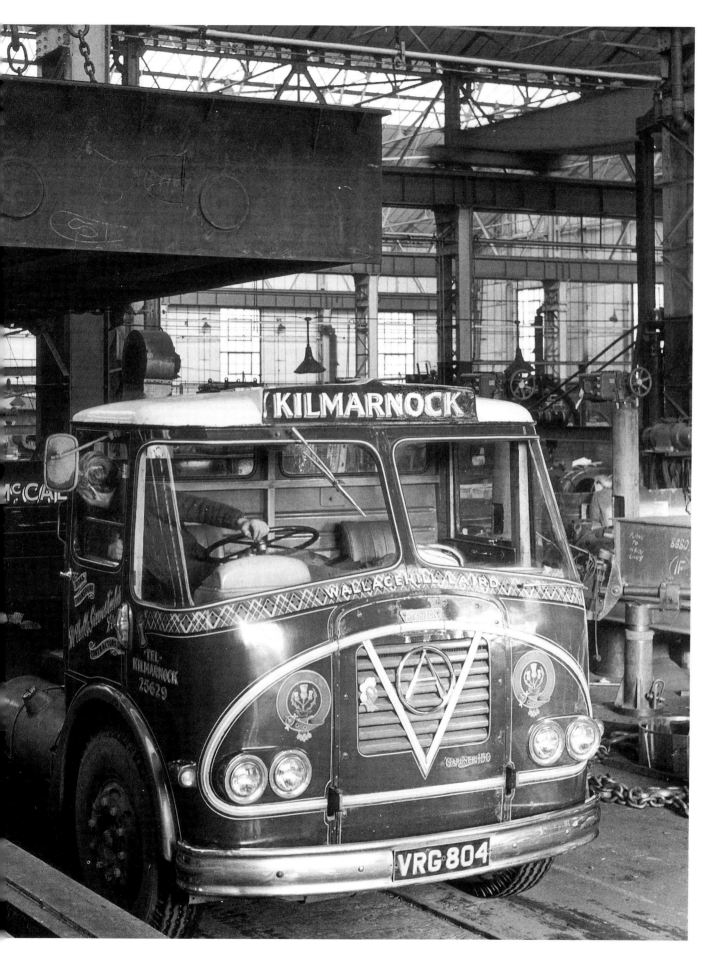

In the annals of Kilmarnock transport folk lore, the standing of John McCall is second to none. Nephew of Alex McCall - McCall & Greenshields - he built his reputation on brilliant expertise. John's fleet of 13 dark brown and red vehicles were all nationalised on April 27, 1949, into Unit B.79 but rather than later come back into haulage, he was to specialise in recovery and crane work from his London Road garage. Pictured about 1938, the Scammell - believed to be UC 1047, which was chassis number 1169 and built in 1928 - is enroute to London complete with roof mounted supplies of petrol. It's load is a 7nhp single cylinder Ransomes, Sims & Jeffries traction engine which was new to James McQuarter of Tradumock near Ayr and later owned by McQuarter Bros of Kirkoswald road, Maybole, who were well known agricultural engineers and contractors. The engine was registered SD 5303 in 1921 and last licensed in 1937.

During war time years, John McCall operated as part of the Ministry of War Transport being Unit 11/Q/21. This line up in his old Riverside garage yard - originally the site of Kilmarnock's Kirkstile pit - demonstrates some of McCall's expertise. Weirs of Glasgow had changed from pump production to gun manufacture and originally loaded three units onto a wagon and trailer combination. John, however, devised a simple system of chocks so that five more guns could be carried on the same outfit. A big lover of AECs, one of his Matadors was to become the BRS Abington breakdown truck after nationalisation. Another AEC - BCS 675 - passed to Pickfords together with BAG 899, a Scammell 20LA low loader. Two McCall drivers in the line up were Jock Smith and Bobby Grant while brothers Jim and Frank MacDougall worked as trailer mates.

William McGillivray started in local haulage at Carlisle during 1924. Joined by his brother John, the partnership expanded by mainly hauling road materials for Cumberland County Council although the two partners sensed long distance work was the way to go. Plaster products to builders and merchants took their fleet of four Foden steamers and five mixed motor vehicles - Albion, Pierce Arrow, Ford and Willys Manchester - as far away as Glasgow and Aberdeen. Seen beside Carlisle Castle decked out for the town's carnival in 1928 are two Foden tippers, the one nearest the camera - 'Enterprise' - being chassis number 13032 and registered HH 4401 when new in 1928. Fleet number 5 is 'Endeavour' and it has John McGillivray at it's wheel whilst brother William is stood beside it. The other men are Phil Scott and Harry Salkeld.

The McGillivrays were keen steam men and between December 1931 and September 1932, they took delivery of four Sentinel DG6 wagons registered HH 6002, 6057, 6190 and 6392. The first of the bunch is seen having just left the manufacturers at Shrewsbury it having maker's number 8636. After an argument, the brothers split up so the directors of Carlisle Plaster & Cement Co stepped in to take over the vehicles. They created Thistle Transport Ltd although by 1933 Thistle had been sold to Alex Smart of Leith. William McGillivray held the job of manager and he was to establish Thistle as a company of high repute. It was only when the problem of death duties arose in 1946 that the assets had to be sold. Rather than allow McGillivray to buy himself back into ownership, the administrators of Thistles sold the 20+ fleet to Robsons of Carlisle.

Geoff Munton's first two haulage vehicles were acquired when he bought a coal round based in the village of Osbournby. The purchase was done in partnership with his brother-in-law Ernie Muxlow, so until Ernie died in 1956, the vehicles were ran under the name of Muxlow & Munton. The fleet increased with the purchase of six ex BRS vehicles from Spilsby about 1954, a method used by many to get started in transport after de-nationalisation. The photograph of the Ruskington depot in Westcliffe Road was taken in 1957 to record Munton's first continental traffic - three loads for the Hanover Trade Fair. LTL 599 was one of three similar FE two stroke powered Foden tractor units then in service recalled for their questionable reliability.

Geoffrey Charles Munton was to become Lincolnshire's leading heavy haulier during the 1950s and '60s although his background was very much amongst the building and civil engineering trade. Prior to World War II he was employed by F Hossock & Son of Ruskington who built the first brick hanger at RAF Cranwell. Being taken prisoner at Singapore, Geoff was to spend more than three years in the POW camps. He weighed less than four stones when liberated in 1945 but it was his mental resolve never to take orders again which meant Geoff became self employed. Returning to the building trade, his investment in heavy plant lead to the purchase of his first low loader and thus the expansion into heavy haulage. This Priestman photograph shows two of Munton's finest loaded with 25 ton face shovels. Long serving driver Bill Carrington is wearing the cap with his back to camera.

Below: Munton's first low loader was not surprisingly a Scammell - although not this one. 659 MMU dates from 1957 and was bought second hand apparently through the Newcastle dealer of Bill Simmons. One of a convoy of three, the Gardner powered artic was driven by Pete Mason and is seen bisecting the town of Brigg enroute from Immingham docks to the slag works at Scunthorpe. Heaviest load in the trio was a 48 ton piece which Henry Dunmore hauled with his Foden 6x4 unit OCT 501. All Munton's vehicles were controlled by transport manager Harold Warrington who joined the firm from BRS Spilsby. Another second hand Scammell bought by Muntons was CSF 272C, a 6x4 Junior Constructor artic.

Following the first trip to Hanover, Munton's evolved into a continental specialist. Geoff Munton ran three articulated fridge vans - the first one being built in his Ruskington yard - carrying supplies from Northern Ireland to the American bases in Germany & France, but it was on the heavy side where Muntons excelled. Henry Dunmore - on the right - and mate Tony Wright are pictured about to leave the depot for Northern Italy. YTL 266 was new in 1964 and sported the Foden two stroke engine. Henry worked at Muntons from 1954 until 1969 and became one of the firm's top low loader drivers. His experience served him well as he established his own continental delivery business which currently sees him delivering items in his 1 ton pick-up as far away as Italy and Spain.

Seen flying the flag during March 1967 are two thirds of a memorable convoy which travelled 1200 miles from Grantham to Turin. The King low loaders were supporting more than £100,000 of machines built by the British Manufacture & Research Co for use in the production of Fiat car bodies. Crossing the channel from Southampton to Le Havre, the Munton trio had a police escort for the entire journey across France to Mont Blanc. Vehicle dimensions were 10' 6" wide and 13' high, the job being done in conjunction with Pickfords.

Below: Pictured leaving the Invicta works at Grantham, Alan Dunmore is loaded with an Aveling Barford road grader destined for delivery to Yugoslavia. More closer to home, Geoff Munton's own plant was involved in a multitude of different jobs during the 1960s. They were part of the team which built the first 100,000 ton tanker berth at Barrow-in-Furness while also building sea defences in Suffolk and fire breaks in Northumberland's Kielder Forest. Muntons diverse itinerary included the construction of the 11 mile stretch of Colsterworth dual carriageway of the A1 and building Ruskington's own secondary school.

Geoff Munton was to favour Foden for more than 20 years with all his new tractors being supplied by Bas Moore of Newark Road Garage in Lincoln. RTL 601J turned out to be his heavyweight swan song although it turned the heads even before it got to work. Used as an exhibit at the 1969 Lincolnshire County Show, the strength of the S40 cab was put to the test when a Mini motor car was placed on the double skin roof. Ron Boddy gave the Foden a lot more care when he was given custody of it although after five years this and the Munton fleet were sold to the P & O Group because of Geoff's failing health and cash flow difficulties. The vehicles were repainted into the blue & white colours of Eastern Roadways and for a year they worked out of the old Munton premises with Harold Warrington and Len Carter being the ex Munton staff who ran their operation.

In his time, William Stephen Nicholson was Cockermouth's foremost transport operator. Unlike some of his counterparts, in 1927 William started with a single horse powered mount and had expanded to three such horse and cart combinations before his first mechanised vehicle - a solid tyred Leyland RM 7126 - was bought on May 26, 1930. A door to door coal round was Nicholsons first work although running from the station to the local gas works was the reason behind the need for greater carrying capacity. Pictured in the town's High Street during the 1930 Carnival, John Graves is the figure leading the horse.

Of all the many assorted Nicholson load carriers, JJ 3372 was something rather special. Built as a dual purpose vehicle, the long wheelbase Bedford tipper was converted - and registered - by Carmichaels of London from a bonneted vehicle to semi-forward control so it's platform area would be increased. With the tipping sides removed, Nicholsons then used a block & tackle to drop a container on it's back and operate it on furniture removals. Seen at New Street in 1932, the figures in shot are eldest son Robert Nicholson - on the tailboard - with his brother William beside him. 12 year old John Nicholson is the face at the driver's window.

Nicholsons first base was at 20 South Street in Cockermouth but when they moved to New Street, William named the residence 'Bedford House' as an indication of how much he liked the marque. Apart from the earlier mentioned Leyland, the only other known interlopers amongst the Bedford regime were FAO 65 and GRM 904, two Seddon four wheeled tippers. Pictured outside the garage is Charlie Lapraik - a man who stayed with Nicholsons for most of his driving life - with his 3 ton short tipper which came new in 1939. Other similar Bedfords bought around that time were CRM 344, 439 and 600 plus DRM 209. The New Street depot was compulsorily acquired when the Nicholson fleet was nationalised into Unit C578.

DAO 884 was also new into service during early 1939, the big attraction to the W series Bedfords being the unladen weight of just under 2ton 10cwt. This meant the vehicle's speed limit was 30mph - 10mph more than vehicles exceeding this weight. Although it bears fleet number 1, Nicholsons ran a large number of Bedfords before this one, some of their early tippers being RM 8929, AAO 83, AAO 292, AAO 658 and ARM 277. John Menhems is the figure in the photograph, his Bedford, like most of the Nicholson fleet - working a great deal for the Keswick Granite Co Ltd.

Originally starting with milk tankers in the Ayrshire village of Trabboch, brothers Bill and Charlie McClelland were occupying new premises in the Heathfield area of Ayr by 1959. A distinct change of traffic took the brothers away from milk onto long distance work and to go with the changing image, the brothers took the name of Oswald from a street name in Ayr, as the title of their new company. The 1960 fleet make up, which was almost 50 strong, saw a dominance of AEC and Atkinson with LCS 729 being one of three AEC Mercury - Dyson 28' artics. JVD 532 was a Gardner 6LW powered Atkinson eight wheeler usually driven by George London - or Wee Yorkie as he was known. HOT 639 had the AEC 9.6 engine and Jock Mackenzie as it's regular driver whilst Ronnie Martin's artic LSO 129 - one of two similar Atkinson outfits - was coupled to a York 33' tandem. The large building behind the company offices formed the workshop and transhipping warehouse.

Oswalds were to run four Leyland Octopus' and a sole Foden but their best remembered eight wheeler must have been OAG 7 - purely because of it's 7.7 litre engine. Fitting the small power pack had been the idea of Charlie McClelland but it was never a success. Regular driver Pat Kane recalls that it was so down on power that running at 24 tons gross felt more like 44 tons. Heading south over Shap took ages whilst northbound up the famous A6 incline seemed to take an eternity. Yard foreman Jackie Fitzsimmons is believed to be the figure shunting the eight wheeler in the premises of Scottish Stampings at Ayr. Fully loaded with 16 pallets - weighing a ton each - of axles, the vehicle would be sheeted before leaving for either Leylands, Fodens or delivery into Fords at either Langley or Woolwich.

It was a rare occurrence to see an Oswald vehicle being overtaken although this shot was specially posed for AEC photographer John Simons who somehow arranged for the presence of Clabens AEC Mammoth Major VRG 207 - chassis number G8RAD2282. The backbone of Oswalds traffic was their overnight trunk which saw 13 drivers leave Ayr every Sunday night first heading for Warrington and then - as roads and vehicles improved - bound for the New Road Cafe on the A34 at Newcastle-under-Lyme. Keeping the Newcastle shunters busy meant 12 more vehicles left Ayr on a Monday night as their compatriots were heading north. CAG 157C was one of six similar AEC Mandators which went on the road in 1965, the year when the McClelland brothers decided to sell out to the GKN Group although the services of Bill & Charlie were retained - as was the Oswald name. Tommy Morrison had this vehicle from new although Bobby Docherty is pictured at the wheel with a load of axles bound for the Albion plant at Scotstoun.

Oswalds main traffic flow was based on three main customers. Scottish Stampings at Ayr produced all manner of axles, half shafts and the like for the motor industry whilst Hoover's Cambuslang factory and Rowweb Building Contractors saw the Oswald vehicles in and out of Glasgow. All Oswald's work was controlled by long serving transport manager Jimmy Cree who was able to give a driver his back load instructions before the first 5p of a long distance telephone call was used up. This particular line up was a one off as the six brand new Weatherill loading shovels are pictured in Peterborough prior to the long haul north to Aberdeen. AEC Mercurys MSD 978 and 977

share the similar design of light alloy cab fitted to Albion Reiver MSD 974 and Albion Chieftan LAG 645. Together with Chieftans JSD 506 and LAG 94, all the vehicles share the distinctive two tone blue livery with Glasgow - London proudly emblazoned to the front. Whilst the Glasgow depot was simply Oswald's presence in the Hoover Cambuslang factory, London related to the Colney Heath premises which incorporated seven beds for visiting scottish men. Drivers in this line up included brothers Bob & Parker Saunders and Dave Muir.

Having a vehicle travel 100,000 miles isn't something which creates much interest in the 1990s but Scania dealership Reliable Vehicles of Glasgow were so pleased with the service from the first tractor they sold in Scotland, they arranged for Ayr photographer George Crawford to take this distinctive photograph. GSD 419E was a constant trunk wagon and so went through many driver's hands. Pat Kane recalls it was a comfortable and lovely vehicle to drive but unlike it's sister Vabis - JCS 835F - it wasn't fitted with a turbocharger and thus wasn't too lively. Pictured with a load of chipboard out of Irvine, the tractor is also recalled for it's very small fuel tank. Many's the time the artic would run out of diesel on the slip road to the Newcastle depot and the driver had to end his journey on foot. GKN eventually phased out the Oswald name and repainted the vehicles in their group colours. Maxi Haulage were to take over these vehicles and work about 1982.

Opposite above: Jabez Oughton gave his name - and some of his money - to the Spennymoor, County Durham based Oughton Carriers when it was established in 1920 although it was his son-in-law, John George Hindmarch (pictured standing) who ran the business. The company's first vehicle was PT 27 - an ex WD chain drive Commer - which was first driven by Bill Christinson, seen on the sturdy mudguard. Oughtons started with a three times a week carrier run between Newcastle and Spennymoor although surmounting Croxdale bank was always a nail biter. One way to ensure the cone clutch kept it's grip was to pour pumice powder into it's innards as the hill started. PT 109 - a solid tyred shaft drive Guy - was Oughton's second vehicle although by 1938 three vehicles were ran. From then until 1946, Oughtons were owned by Film Transport Services but bought back into family ownership, Oughtons have continued to provide a north east delivery service. John's son Barrie now runs an 11 strong fleet which is based in Chilton.

Opposite below: William Proudman was to apparently clock up almost 1.25 million miles behind the wheel of his 1932 Leyland Badger RF 9571 in the 30 years he had the 5 tonner in service. Pictured in the works of Smiths Asbestos at Tamworth, loads out of here took William as far away as London at a top speed of no more than 38mph. Another long running contract was collecting cattle feed from Frodsham in Cheshire to deliver back into the Tamworth branch of Staffordshire Farmers. Still being started on the handle, the petrol engined Badger was traded in to Brownshill Motor Sales during 1962 in part exchange for a second hand Leyland Comet. Chassis number 18554 was subsequently bought by Paul Adams who's restored the Badger to Concours condition, it winning the trophy for the best Leyland on the 1993 London - Brighton run.

Paying £25 for this 1962 Albion Claymore was reckoned to be the best money Sandy Reive has ever spent even though at the time it didn't have a body and it's four cylinder engine was seized. The vehicle had been owned by Federated Foundries of Glasgow although operated through a subsidiary - Thames Bank Iron Company - in London. Pictured outside Moffat Co-op on a removals job, the vehicle was normally driven by Bert Nicoll on a coal round out of Abington station. In partnership with David Grossart, Sandy went on to form Reive & Grossart - a company which Sandy now owns himself. Moving from Leadhills to Abington, Sandy currently operates a 13 strong fleet which is ERF dominated.

Up until 1928, Ezra Claude Human worked in a garage but he was persuaded to go into haulage by a local potato merchant. Based at Terrington St Clement, just west of Kings Lynn, Ezra's first vehicle was a Manchester and he gradually built up to a fleet of a dozen under the name of Reliance Transport. He took the title from a coach concern which was ran by a relative in Grantham. Hauling mainly agricultural produce traffic, London was to be his first destination with return loads of meal out of Silcocks taking him back to the local farms. AVF 310 came new in 1936, it's first tilt body being put on during the fruit season when chips of strawberries were delivered up to Nelson and Blackpool. The Bedford was ran throughout the war time years and was relegated to the fleet hack which all the new starters had to cut their teeth on. Ezra's favourite remark if anyone complained about defects with AVF was "Don't you know there's a war on."

About 1931 Ezra bought an aircraft hanger and had it erected in the centre of the village by the local carpenter and builder. It became policy that all the vehicles were parked inside the hanger when back at base on a night. The fleet was a mixture of Bedford, Morris and Thornycrofts although the flagship, seen at the back, was the AEC Matador Mk II four wheeler and drawbar trailer outfit CNP 473 usually driven by George Kingston. CNG 579 and CPW 377 are the two pictured Morris Commercial Equaload four wheelers which were usually driven by Horace Human and Sid Cornwell. The vehicles were only a year old when war broke out and both they and their respective drivers were commandeered to Colchester for military service. Other Morris' being ran in 1939 included CAH 814 - a similar four wheeler - and CVF 238, an artic unit coupled to a Carrimore semi-trailer which was usually driven by Bert Rae.

FNG 20 was one of three Vulcans ran by Reliance it being new in 1945. Their first Vulcan was EPW 879 and it was collected new from the Maidstone factory in 1944 by Reliance driver Jim Lane who happened to be home on wartime leave at the time. Whilst the first two were petrol powered, the third - KVF 704, new in 1949 - had the Perkins P6 engine. The Vulcan shares the photograph with driver Raymond Rowley Rudd - always known as Sam - who started at Reliance in 1936 as a driver's mate. Both he and the Vulcan were soon to be part of British Road Services when Ezra's entire operation was taken over. More than 40 years on the old Reliance hanger is currently in use as a furniture warehouse.

John Rhind didn't come into road haulage until about 1954. The son of an Aberdeenshire farmer (Mains of Auchnagatt) his first vehicles were five cattle floats bought from Leiths Transport of Froghall Road in Aberdeen. John took over these premises as well although he soon set his sights on general haulage and phased the cattle wagons out. HRG 866 - chassis number 3871H2002 - dates from 1955 and had Morrison Taylor as it's regular driver. Hidden beneath the sheets is a part load of eggs which Rhinds hauled from the Maud grading station. Consignments of this traffic were ran regularly to London and Reading whilst a night trunk carried eggs to Glasgow.

Buying vehicles and licences from wherever he could, JHL 766 came to Aberdeen via Comberhill Garages of Wakefield. The Rhind fleet engineer Bill Dey recalls this Atkinson eight wheeler was always known as the mongrel. When the original Gardner engine blew up with a conrod through the crankcase, a new Gardner was considered to be too expensive. The hard working Rhind fitters transplanted a Leyland 600 engine and gearbox - removed from a smashed up Octopus - then re-aligned the propshaft to suit. The Leyland radiator was also fitted with it's distinctive filler cap being the give away to it's highly successful internal surgery. Jock Angus was the Atky's usual driver and it's load is believed to be frozen fish from Allen & Day in Aberdeen.

LRG 882 dates from 1958 and bore chassis number 3872H2263. Pictured with a load of paper from Muggiemoss Mill in Aberdeen, the Mammoth Major had George Garden as it's first driver. George recalls the bespectacled John Rhind was a good boss to work for. At times impulsive, it wasn't unknown for him to leap on the back of a wagon and assist loading boxes of fish before realising he had his best suit on. When George eventually left Rhinds to set up on his own with a filling station, he approached John to voice his apprehension over the viability of his new project. To help him on his way, John arranged for every Rhind company car to always fill up at George's new garage and pay for the fuel promptly.

Roger Kenny found NKW 877 loaded with cattle hides, a regular traffic from the abattoirs of Aberdeen to tanneries at Hull, Beverley, Liverpool, Runcorn and Warrington. Jock Whyte was this AEC's regular driver, the eight wheeler - chassis number 3871H1932 - being bought by Rhinds from the Aberdeen haulier Andy Geddis. The 9.6 litre engined vehicle is recalled for the strange idiosyncrasy of it's rear bogie. When reversing from a high camber road into premises - even Rhinds own workshops - the balance beam suspension could tip over and lift the lead driving axle off the road bringing the vehicle to a halt as it lost it's drive.

Pictured by Roger Kenny unloading in Manchester, OLL 913 dates from 1954, it starting life with British Road Services. One of JR's early vehicles, the Leyland's first Aberdeen paint was dark grey and applied by hand. A coat of varnish finished off the Rhind sign writing which was applied by the expert hand of Gibby Morris. The face behind the wheel is believed to be Alec Wilkie, his Gray & Adams manufactured container having sides of beef inside. When Rhinds first began hauling out of the Aberdeen killing houses, they simply used flat bodied vehicles to carry beef which was wrapped in muslin cloth. As the hygiene requirements were uprated, vans then internally racked fridge vans were introduced which finally had to be strengthend as hanging loads became the norm.

Rhinds ran about 10 four wheelers on long distance work. The first ones were bonneted Leyland Comets and Albion Chieftans with coach built cabs made by David Grant of Aberdeen. RRG 419 sports a standard Albion cab which was normally occupied by driver George Cummings. It dates from 1961, the year when John Rhind moved into large premises on South Anderson Drive. Built as an ice rink and sports complex, the building was damaged during the war and the project never completed. Having outgrown Froghall Street and offices in Pittodrie Street, the new premises were also used for warehousing, especially for Fisons fertiliser.

SRG 698 was one of the four Albion Reivers ran by Rhinds - PRS 753 and SRG 699 being two of the others - this one normally having George Wilson at it's wheel. Rated quite highly, the Leyland 400 engine was felt to be slightly down on power when running at full weight. Not surprisingly Rhinds carried a lot of fish traffic, especially in the herring season, from west coast ports like Ullapool down to Great Yarmouth. They only had the one outbased office - in Tower Bridge Road, London - and drivers running elsewhere were expected to find their own back loads through clearing houses or from other hauliers.

George Christie was the normal driver of TRS 267, the Albion Reiver dating from 1962. The load in this Roger Kenny photograph has come from Trollop & Colls in Aberdeen. Rhinds hauled these pipes all over the country although as the hydro-electric schemes were developed in Scotland, some testing drops were requested. One particular delivery point at the top of the Perthshire hills could only be reached by the company's old square cab'd Leyland Octopus. Apparently it was it's large brass helical gear differential which made all the difference in it being able to surmount the terrain.

DRS 167C was one of four similar Albion Clydesdale artic tractor units - one of the others being BRG 573B - which were operated by Rhinds, coupled to Scammell semi-trailers. Pictured with a mixed load of potatoes and paper, Geordie Fyffe was this vehicle's normal driver. As well as his haulage firm, John Rhind also had four or five farms and a car hire business. By 1965 his finances had become over stretched so he sold a controlling share of the haulage operation to another Aberdeen haulier, Charles Alexander & Partners. John Rhind stayed on to manage the firm and for about two years it remained business as usual.

Opposite: Together with the similar VRG 988, this Power Plus range Octopus - chassis number 629192 - was supplied new through Millburn Motors of Glasgow. George Garden got the vehicle new in 1962, it being pictured with a good 15 ton of paper reels on it's back. As well as regular south bound traffic, paper was also carried back to Aberdeen for the local newspapers. However once the Rhind warehousing complex was created, it was usually Fisons fertiliser or Bibbys feed going into store which proved to be ideal backload traffic.

Below: HRG 862E - chassis number 701768 - was the first of nine Ergomatic cab'd Leyland Octopus' which were recalled by the workshops staff as being a mechanically sound batch. Pictured with a load of fertiliser, it's regular driver was Sandy Lowrie. About 1967, Charles Alexanders were bought by Transport Development Group so John Rhind had little option but to sell the minor shareholding of his old company to TDG. Amongst Rhinds last new vehicles were eight Leyland Beaver artic units, these including KRG 965F. Then operating a fleet of 52 strong, Rhinds were to be merged with Pattersons - a subsidiary of Charles Alexanders until bought by TDG - and it's identity lost. By 1984 Pattersons too had been lost when a TDG re-shuffle absorbed their operations into Sutherlands. Although John Rhind had been asked to stay in '67, he left to follow other interests which included sand & gravel work, his farms and a butchery business.

Now operating a high profile fleet counted at 60 strong, the Norfolk concern of J.W. Richards is well known throughout the UK. John William - but always known as Jack - Richards started haulage fairly modestly and for the six years at the start of the '50s, drove for Darby's Sand & Gravel of Sutton in Cambridgeshire. This family business ran 40-50 tippers although Jack's four wheeler - HRY 542 - belied it's true origins. Leaving the Foden factory about 1934, Darby's bought the tipper - together with sister ERF HRY 543 - from the three Murphy brothers of Thurmaston. The famous Leicester company were quite adept at refurbishing 16 year old chassis' into as new condition before re-registering them. Jack recalls the four pot Gardner tipper would only do 29 mph but was still capable of carrying a good 10 ton payload.

After scraping a stake together in 1956, Jack bought himself an 'O' type Bedford through a dealer in London primarily for it's carriers licence. Within a few months the licence was transferred onto KVJ 188 - a second hand petrol engined S type Bedford which had started life with Lucozade. It was to be the original owner's striking yellow colour scheme which Jack adopted and retained for himself - albeit in a slightly amended shade. After an initial good influx of work, Jack found loads starting to dry up so he decided the only way to establish himself was in giving a regular service. Nottingham market every night was the destination Jack offered to the local flower and produce growers around Haddenham in Cambridgeshire and work soon took off again prompting the purchase of two more Bedfords. John Hobson - later to become a manager at Richards - and Eddie Moden were to be the first two employed driving staff. OJE 332 - Richards first brand new vehicle and supplied by Murkitts of Cambridge - had the Bedford diesel engine whilst the second hand NUT 996 had the P6 Perkins.

In search of greater carrying capacity,
Jack bought his first Albion in 1959
and it's believed to have been the first
6x4 Reiver out of the factory fitted
with a limited slip differential. Jack
actually went to Glasgow by train to
collect his new vehicle although in
service Arthur Jackson was it's regular
driver. Usually carrying tomatoes and
cucumbers from Hoddesdon to
Nottingham, Arthur is recalled as
being one of the hardest working
drivers you could wish to employ.
Two other early members of the
driving staff were the clean and
immaculate Sam Giddins plus the ex
professional boxer Maurice Murfitt.
Both characters in their own right, the
pair were featured in the Birmingham
Post as for some reason they delivered
produce into the local market while
wearing black bowler hats.

Richards went into articulation about 1962 as the six carrier's licences bought from Steve Brown of Soham were attached to a mixture of Bedford, BMC and Dodge tractor units. Sporting the rather special Scammell automatic coupling, the universal use of these units was soon to be superseded by the arrival of the fifth wheel coupling. GEW 777D was Richards first conventional artic - one of about six Albions then in service - the Clydesdale tractor unit and BTC 4 in line semi-trailer combining to give a very light outfit.

Into the 1960s, the growing Richards fleet served even more Midlands destinations as the wording on these sideboards indicate. Having just been freshly painted by Swainlands of Cambridge - including the message on the tail board saying Richards Reliable Road Services - this Perkins engined Dodge was actually about three years old. Jack had bought the 1960 vehicle together with it's important carriers licence from George Hitchens of Soham. Although George wanted to get out of haulage, he did do some part time driving for Richards, not particularly on his old Dodge as this vehicle was normally driven by Eric Cavalero.

By the late 1960s Richards seasonal produce traffic was being augmented by heavier general haulage work. Seen loaded with bricks, the Perkins V8.150 powered HEW 609F was one of four similar Seddon -York outfits which were ran up to 28 tons gross. Jack recalls it was price which first attracted him to the Seddon range which was supplied through Sellers & Batty. In 1962 his first Seddon four wheeler, bodied, painted, signwritten and taxed for 12 months was to cost less than £2,000. By 1969 the Richards fleet was counted at 27 strong, 17 of which were Perkins powered.

With such strong sign writing based on a distinctive yellow livery, Jack Richards could never be said to have sought anonymity as this pair of brand new Leyland Boxers aptly demonstrate. Usually driven by the Driver brothers - Richard & Les or Duzzer as he was known - the four wheelers were supplied by Marshalls of Cambridge in 1971. The year of their arrival coincided with the time when Richards adopted Limited status and Jack made the decision to base five vehicles at Fakenham in Norfolk. Within six years the old Haddenham depot had been closed and what started as a 1.5 acre base was set to grow into Richards current six acre HQ.

Historically the Ridings of Longridge near Preston were farming people and hauling coal from the station to the local gas works by horse and cart was only done when the farm was quiet. James Riding bought his first mechanised vehicle in 1922 from Tommy Cunliffe. The seller spent two hours with James to show him how to drive his Karrier lorry and explain about the business of road transport. Initially James' efforts weren't too successful until his father William decided to join him in partnership during 1924 and the W & J Riding title was coined. The pair were then to buy their first Leyland from Tillotsons at Burnley although TC 6143 came later and is pictured in 1936 heading down the A59 at Tarleton for it's next load in Liverpool. The driver is the long serving Arthur 'Tiny' Edelston who was to become a foreman during the time of BRS and continued in this capacity until retirement in 1976 after more than 40 years service. The company had soon latched onto drawbar trailers - of Dyson and Atkinson manufacture - to increase capacity, this Leyland expected to haul all of 12 tons payload.

Ridings expanded in their earliest days carrying Preston Farmer's traffic with regular back loads including wheat from Yorkshire and fish meal from BOCM at Hull. RJ 258 however is loaded with about 14 tons of alum blocks from Peter Spence Ltd at Widnes. Due to the shortage of vehicles during the War, Ridings bought this Leyland Hippo as a burnt out wreck from Dallas of Leyland. The model TSW 1 was chassis number 67816 and started life in November 1931 with Wolfendale of Swinton. Ridings re-built the six wheeler although fitted an 8.6 litre diesel in place of the original petrol one together with a larger radiator. Harold Bristow was the regular driver of the vehicle which was known as 'The Crab' because of it's difficulty to steer. Matters weren't enhanced by the fitment of K type wheels which were liable to wobble unless fitted spot on. The Hippo was capable of 37mph because of a booster gearbox fitment although this also created a screaming noise from the transmission.

Ran on contract to the Bold Venture Lime Co to carry tarmac for road construction work, this pair of Leyland Lynxs had a long and varied life with Ridings. Bought ex WD, the haulier converted them first into hydraulic tippers. Driver of GTE 515 was Tommy Smith whose grandson is now a driver at Ridings. Harold Bristow wanted more time for his darts nights so he came off long distance work to take GTE 516. Both vehicles were converted from petrol to diesel when Leyland Comet 350 power packs were inserted along with five speed gearboxes and two speed axles. Eventually stretched to long wheelbase platforms, they were to be re-registered RTD 173 and RTC 914. These two vehicles along with the rest of the ten strong Riding fleet were to be compulsorily acquired in the wave of nationalisation.

November 8, 1954, was a memorable day in the Riding calendar as this saw the premises and fleet pass back from BRS into family ownership. Although William was to take no furthur part in the business, his son James decided to keep the old W & J title. The first two ex BRS vehicles painted back into Riding blue - a week premature to the actual sale date - were KKA 486 - a six wheeled Hippo chassis number 485789 which started life in 1948 with W Lewis of Liverpool and was soon to be converted into an eight wheeler - and ABV 602, Ridings one and only ERF eight legger.Carrying Tate & Lyle sugar east and ICI products west, the ERF was worked on the overnight trunk to Darlington. Ridings were to employ the ex BRS staff of Frank Ferguson as depot manager and Frank Ross as foreman driver, to establish their north east depot. In a Leyland dominated firm the ERF was soon to be part exchanged and in it's place came the two year old ex Chester Farmer's Octopus NFM 205.

Although James Riding had been employed as a BRS depot manager, like many in the same position he had longed for denationalisation to dawn. In buying up the Burnley based Queensgate Motors Ltd he had been quietly running two vehicles, a year before the old Riding fleet could be re-purchased. Even after the sale went through, the establishing of certain contracts meant the Queensgate name was retained for more than 10 years. Seen loaded with ICI PVC products, Leyland Beaver GLV 507 dates from 1946, it being the first vehicle purchased with and for it's 'S' licence after denationalisation had started. Driver Dick Robinson (Uncle Dick) had joined Ridings from a local firm called John Taylors in 1932 especially to drive a diesel engined Leyland Buffalo. He was the first driver of Ridings to be re-employed after denationalisation. The Beaver had chassis number 461394 and was new to Union Road Transport of Liverpool.

Pictured outside Riding's Daniel Platt garage at Longridge, VTB 954 was to be the company's third and last Bedford, the other two having come with the purchase of the Queensgate Motors business. This S type had originally been a Leyland Motors experimental vehicle trying out the early fitment of the Comet 350 engine into the Bedford chassis. The new 'whistler' power pack meant the four wheeler could go like a march hare but the rest of the transmission was rather unreliable. Tom Riding recalled that the gearbox and rear axle used to alternate on a three monthly failure. Jimmy Lomas was the vehicle's regular driver and it's pictured with a load of trichloroethylne.

Ridings were to get sterling service from many of their Leylands not least of which was WTF 574. Together with the similar Leyland Octopus XTB 198, fleet number 24 with chassis number 551971 was new in 1955 and ran almost non stop for 10 years. Hardly bothered with this spectacular flood near Otley, the Octo model 240/4 was brought into the garage in 1965 when it was totally refurbished. It had a furthur five years of work ahead of it before being pensioned off in 1970.

It became Riding policy that for a brand new vehicle's first 1,000 miles, it would only be given light loads to carry. Fresh from the 1959 Royal Lancashire Show, 200 KTE has thus a modest load of cigarettes inside this Anglo - Continental container collected from Preston docks and destined for London. Together with sister vehicle 375 HTB, this four wheeler was found to have too heavy an unladen weight. Soon converted with a York third axle into a 14 ton payload carrying six wheeler, the Leyland proved more viable on the north east trunk service. Margaret Ball - later to become Mrs Tom Riding - is sharing the photograph with the gleaming Super Comet which bore the chassis number 594684.

When buying new, Ridings endeavoured to match the registration numbers of a vehicle to the size of it's engine so 680 ETJ was fitted with a Leyland 680 engine. New in 1958, the vehicle started life as a four wheeled rigid hauling a drawbar trailer. Dick Walton - he retired from Ridings in 1992 - was the vehicle's regular driver and he was obliged to adapt to it's conversion into a four axled artic. In order to quell any early fears that rigid drivers had over jackknifing artics, Ridings worked closely with Westinghouse over the fitment of load sensing devices for the air brake systems long before the industry as a whole had heard of them.

After serving his apprenticeship with Lcyland Motors and two years National Service in the RAF, Riding's current MD Tom Riding came into the business during 1956. Together with his elder brother, who was named after their father James, the three worked together until James senior decided to sell out to the Transport Development Group in 1970. Tom had soon decided that articulation was the way to go although his father was to take some convincing. The company's first artic was a Leyland Comet 700 KTE which was recalled as poor on power and brakes. At first James senior didn't want Tom to get any heavyweight Leyland artic units although he did allow this 470 engined AEC Mercury onto the fleet in 1960. OTB - 'Our Tom's Baby' - was bought new from Tillotsons but in less than a week it was towed back for a new engine when the cylinder liner seals failed. Regular driver of the AEC was Ted Woods - still on the Riding staff in 1993 - and he was to get a reconditioned engine or short motor for the Mercury every year of it's life, such was it's poor reliability.

In search of a lighter unladen weight, Ridings took their first Mark 1 Atkinson tractor unit - 6520 TF - about 1962. Gardner 150 powered ATB 150A came in 1963 and was given to Tommy Lambert. Riding's last Leyland was to be YTD 360D and although it gave good service, Atkinson then Seddon Atkinson became a company favourite. 1993 fleet size is around the 95 mark and Ridings tend to work 'the golden triangle' - between Longridge, Thornaby in the north east and Glasgow - as it's a traffic office expression that England ends at Birmingham. Scottish work was initially started through the clearing house of David Vetters although Ridings were to get a lot of Turner's asbestos pipe traffic and work directly for British Steel out of all the Scottish steel works.

Now into their third generation, the Hornsby family owned Ryton Sand & Gravel concern has been active in the north east for more than 50 years. Their first vehicles were predominantly Commer and Albion four wheelers although Leyland have long been and are currently still favoured. HCN 177G was one of four similar Leyland Octopus' based at Rothbury, the Caistron quarry being known for it's red sand and gravel extraction from the Coquet river. Raymond Watson was the regular driver of this tipper which was fitted with Neville Charrold body and lifting rams.

Charles Bisset was a sub contractor who ran exclusively in Ryton's distinctive livery and during the 1950s and '60s had a fleet of five short wheelbase tippers at work including 489 UP which he drove. Leyland Comets DNL 806 and ETY 492 were Comet 75s working out of Crawcrook quarry whilst OPT 113 and HTY 866 were Comet 90s of 1953 and '54 vintage working out of Merryshields quarry. OPT is recalled for it's specially built low line forward control cab made by JS Robson of Consett so it could get under a low gravel hopper at Merryshields. Other Comets of the mid 1950s were KTY 443 and MTY 886 - both of which worked out of Caistron - while the small TK Bedford 3624 PT new in 1963 worked out of Crawcrook. Roy Bisset - Charlie's son - currently runs two Volvos on contract to Tilcon.

Like most in the sand and gravel business, Ryton expanded through buying up smaller operations. West Tyne Gravel, Merryshield S & G and Hexham Riverside S & G being three such concerns. MCN 254K was based at Hedgeley quarry, Powburn, Wooler. This Ryton base doesn't actually extract anything on site as current company drivers like Harry Clark bring the ballast from the Ingram valley in the Cheviots for crushing and washing at Hedgley. The Gardner 6LXB-180 powered Foden was normally driven by Jimmy Fogan. Ryton currently run a fleet of about 25 strong which is Volvo dominated.

In 1935 Jack Sanderson was selling petrol at 1/3d (6p) a gallon from Central Garage in Loftus but he also ran a Morris Commercial and two 2 ton Fordsons mainly on work for North Yorkshire County Council. Together with the similar four wheeler VN 9269 - which was driven by Kell Brown - this two tonner came new in 1937 being supplied through one Mr Sano, the Middlesbrough International dealer. The Wood Hoist equipped underbody tipper was given new to Peter Johnson who recalled it's regular 4 ton payload earned him £2.25 a week. Seen at South Bank gas works, it's load of coke is destined for the brazier fires at Birk Brow dual carriageway road works. Powered by the four cylinder petrol engine, the International managed awkward climbs like the haul out of Grosmont brick yard because of it's two speed rear axle.

On the outbrcak of hostilities, Sandersons were to loose an almost new Bedford and a Commer when commandeered for Army use. Their Albion - VN 9704 - and one of the Bedfords - GHN 184 - was ran exclusively for the Ministry of War Transport but after his National Service, Peter Johnson got HUP 255 new in 1947. Fitted with Edbro twin ram tipping gear, it's pictured on some urgent coke haulage when a rail strike threatend production at Skinningrove steel works. The steel maker fabricated the oversize greedy boards although even here - having just left Fishburn coke works - the Bedford isn't even close to it's five ton capacity.

Due to their localised operations Sandersons missed out on nationalisation and the fleet was to peak around the 23 mark in 1960. Jack's sons Austin and Leo were to come into the business and ran it until their retirement in the late '60s. Post war vehicles included many ex War Department although perhaps non more stranger than an ex RAF Thornycroft. When you looked under the bonnet there was just an empty space as the engine was located in the cab. The specially built vehicle had originally been fitted with a generator under the bonnet but this had been removed prior to the sale. JAJ 176 was new in 1952 and given to the long serving Peter Johnson who took this photograph as he tipped a load of tarmac chippings into the council stockyard at Fridaythorpe - midway between Malton and Driffield. Even though the petrol engined S type Bedford 7 tonner had fixed sides on it's tipper body, Peter had to run across to Hull for a back load of cattle feed before returning home.

Working with North Yorkshire County Council involved Sandersons with all manner of road construction projects although the most testing of these must have been the fortnight spent on Sutton Bank during 1953. Such is the incline - 1 in 3 at it's worst - on the A170 between Thirsk and Helmsley as it surmounts the famous Whitestonecliffe, contractors had to approach the bank from two different directions. For work below the tight hairpin tippers approached from Thirsk although when re-surfacing was being done on the top of the climb, vehicles came via Helmsley and reversed down to the hair pin. Hauling the tarmac laying Barber Green up Sutton Bank took the combined efforts of the County Council's 6x6 Mack and their long serving Foden steamer, taking turns to either winch or act as anchor. Bill Rennie is the Foden driver in black overalls stood in front of the Mack with him being the Northallerton based Harry Hall who was in charge of the Council's transport. The petrol engined Mack was normally based at Whitby and during winter months was used as a snow plough. To ensure it held it's weight as a winch vehicle, the tilt bodywork hides the fact it was ballasted with a load of chippings. Wilf Readman is driving the Sanderson's O type whilst Peter Johnson is at the wheel of his S type Bedford.

It was during the 1930s that Ted Greenwood, Chilly Everdell and the Darby family got together to form a sand & gravel concern. This partnership, however, was not to last so as well as his road haulage interests, Ted Greenwood set up St Ives Sand & Gravel in 1938. The Cambridgeshire concern soon expanded, an early fleet line up showing a predominance of 'O' series Bedfords. The six wheelers were of International manufacture and are recalled for their left hand drive steering position. When early drivers like Joe Spencer wanted to indicate he was turning right, he used a stick with a dummy hand on the end to push out the offside window and show his intentions.

By the late 1950s a view of the St Ives West End yard shows the inroads which Foden had made into the fleet although perhaps the most interesting part of the photograph is the top right line up in the graveyard. VEW 641 was a Gardner 6LW powered eight wheeler although two of the company's half cab mixers were two stroke powered. St Ives operated early Rapier and Stothert & Pitt drums which being powered by donkey engines meant they were a self contained unit. Due to the expertise of fitting staff like Tug Wilson and Stan Norman, what was a tipper today could be a mixer tomorrow. It was a four hour job for three men to remove the tipping mechanism and body from a Foden eight wheeler then replace it with one of the seven or eight spare mixers kept for such demands.

As well as running tippers and mixers, St Ives also ran a number of platform vehicles to deliver pipes, kerbstones, slabs and other pre-cast concrete products. In 1960 it was a fairly standard practice to use one of their five eight wheelers like this 1950 AEC Mammoth Major together with an independent bogie to handle 40 ton beams. Pictured having just left the Meadows Lane plant at St Ives, the crew's greatest difficulty was in lining up the ex WD bogie. Destined for Hills Road railway bridge in Cambridge, the outfit's first problem was in just getting out of St Ives. Even with an escort in the firm's Ford Thames van, clearing the corner at Kiddle's furniture shop took it's toll in sweat.

St Ives ran about 40 of these S20 Foden eight wheelers, the first with the Gardner 6LWs and the latter six with the 6LX-150 engines. SEW 796 came new in 1957 and was regularly driven by Fred Britten, one of the company's cream drivers. Seen in front of the old West End gravel pit, the eight wheeler was fitted with Pilot tipping gear. St Ives specified two different types of transmissions to their S20s. In place of the five speed gearbox, some of the eight wheelers had the two stick 12 speed transmission. This spread of performance meant they could also be used on towing duties. Rather than have a ballast box tractor unit, St Ives preferred to use loaded eight wheelers to move their assorted mobile crushers, fuel bowsers and auxiliary plant.

Mark 5 AEC Mandator 285 LEW was operated out of the company's concrete products division, there being about 12 tons in these 50' long hollow section box beams destined to be used in the construction of the M1 motorway. Regular drivers of this AEC were Mick Woods - who still works out of the St Ives plant - and Bernie Dalton. The bogie was a BTC 4 in line and although it was far more modern than it's ex WD counterpart, the 1968 plating & testing regulations proved it's downfall as the required braking efficiency could never be reached. St Ives replaced these load supporters with tandem axle Dyson units.

St Ives were to run about 10 of these Ergomatic cab'd AEC Mammoth Majors with the 691 engines and six speed gearboxes. The eight wheeler is seen under the old Meadow Lane bins which offered 6mm, 10mm, 20mm or 40mm sizes of gravel. Regular driver of this vehicle was Ernie Hobbs who together with George Rignell were classed as the company's two old & trusted retainers. Prior to the requirement for an MoT plate in 1968, all the St Ives tipper bodies were obliged to be fitted with internal calibration stripes. By using these - linked to the type of product being carried - the true weight of the load could be calculated.

The bridge over the River Ouse at St Ives has been linking Bridge Street to London Road since around the 12th century. It's width is rather restrictive for 20th century traffic and this is what occurred when driver Jerry Dalton had to take action and avoid a wandering pedestrian. Works manager Geordie Morris required the use of 179 BEW - the company's Foden eight wheeled mobile crane - to lift the half cab tipper clear of the drop. The wrecker at the rear is 'Gertie', an AEC Matador which St Ives ran on trade plates 007 EW. The only repairs needed to the Neville bodied Foden was to re-adjust the steering's tracking. The biggest expense of the incident was in having to hire the police diving team to recover all the stones prior to re-building the bridge into it's original condition.

Those who were to know Ted Greenwood as a marvellous boss were to mourn his death in 1967. The St Ives concern was bought for £8 million by Consolidated Goldfields who in 1969 also bought up Amalgamated Roadstone. Two years later, Consolidated bought the Amey Group and the ARC title was to be coined for all the group's roadstone interests. The passage of time saw a variety of liveries and Geordie Morris recalls how one vehicle had three different paint jobs in three weeks. Pictured at the Ely pre-mix plant, the ex St Ives half cab is seen in it's last ARC colours. Fred Wadlow is pictured at the door although old St Ives men will note 'Flower Pot', the S21 Foden on the left of shot as it was the only company Foden mixer fitted with this distinctive full cab.

Smiths of Eccles can trace their roots back to 1910 and although the company bears the name of George Smith, the firm was owned by the Rouse family as far back as anyone can remember. Roy Woodward Rouse left his job as a journalist to take over the business from his father around 1934 operating from Belmont Garage in Monton at Eccles. Leyland Octopus DJ 7557 - chassis number 14238, model TEW9T, new to Davies & Brownlow of St Helens - is seen during wartime years, it was the 33rd vehicle to be acquired as it became company policy to only use a fleet number once. Like most long distance operations, Smiths were a prime candidate for nationalisation although R W Rouse sold out voluntarily around 1948. He was given a District Manager's post at BRS but he soon left this to take up fresh business interests.

By 1954 R W Rouse was back in haulage although due to legal reasons he wasn't allowed to resurrect the old George Smith (Eccles) Ltd title. As an alternative the name Smiths of Eccles was created although HQ wasn't to be in Eccles but on the edge of the Trafford Park industrial estate at Taylor Road in Urmston. Smiths were to be one of the pioneers of Continental transport with their first driver accompanied load being in 1957. A couple of years later they were asked to move part of a linear accelerator from Metropolitan Vickers (now GEC) to the Cern research establishment at Geneva. Crossing the water between Tilbury and Antwerp was done on the Atlantic Steam Navigation Co's "Empire Celtic". Such was the delicate nature of the load, the customer insisted on a 15 mph maximum speed all the way to Switzerland. The trilby wearing onlookers watching Ted Trainer check the clearance on George Gregory's Leyland are R W Rouse and the company's general manager Fred Tessyman. Malcolm Wilford's research dates KKF 715 from 1949, the 12B/1 Beaver being chassis number 494453 and new to Union Road Transport of Liverpool.

Opposite: This impressive 1959 line up of five Leyland Comets and six Albion Chieftans shows part of the contract fleet ran by Smiths on DCL work. In the heady days of 'A' licensing, it was far easier to obtain Contract 'A' licences although this meant the vehicles involved could only carry goods for one named customer. Smiths also ran six Foden tankers - three eight wheelers and three artics - on this carbon dioxide traffic, they being recalled for their heavy unladen weight of 16 tons each. First into service during 1961, the Fodens ran at 24 tons gross but after extending the tractor's wheelbase during 1965, changes in the law meant the artics could run at 28 tons for the last six years of their life. Smiths operated the DCL contract until 1983, the year when TDG decided to merge Smiths with Harris Road Services.

Below: Bought during 1957, Smiths 130th vehicle was 553 DTB - chassis number 572232 - one of 10 Leyland Beaver tractor units which were taken on during the transition from rigids to articulation. Although only having four wheels in line, the legal interpretation at the time of the BTC 26' long flat trailer was that it had two axles. As the cab lettering denotes, Smiths were to establish a network of depots, the London operation being created when the company took over Mountfields of Barking. Smiths in turn were to be acquired by the Transport Development Group in 1961 although R W Rouse stayed on until 1975 when he handed over the post of Managing Director to Don Parkin. Regular driver of this 600 engined Beaver was Trevor Thrush, well known at Smiths for his tall story telling.

Smiths carried literally hundreds of these loads of boiler tubing to power stations all over England from Blyth in the north east to Kingsnorth in Kent. At 18' wide, a load - depending on it's gauge - could weigh up to 14 tons. Fleet number 116 was one of a number of Gardner 6LW powered ERF flats ran by Smiths which at times were expected to haul a drawbar trailer at 32 tons gross. Heavy going for a 112 bhp engine although in later years these ERFs were converted into tankers. The seasonal aspect of their black oil traffic meant they could stand idle in the yard for six months of the year. Smith's HQ was next door to one of Pickfords tanker depots - seen in the background - these premises now being used by the NFC's Tankfreight operation.

Smiths ran about 30 Gardner engined four wheeled flats on multi-drop general haulage work between the north west and midland depots. Predominantly 4LW & 5LW powered ERFs, 166 was their sole Foden which was bought second hand specifically for it's Special 'A' licence. Regular driver of this vehicle being Ted 'Porky' Johnson, shop steward at Smiths for many years, who disliked the Foden for it's excess lean to the nearside on it's rear under slung springs. Sneaking into shot is 106 - NER 370 - one of the ERF eight wheeled black oil tankers with a rare oval grilled cab - a forerunner to the famous KV version.

The Leyland marque was to give Smiths excellent service until the arrival of the Power Plus range about 1961. 198, 200 & 202 were identical Beaver tractors having the 140 bhp version of the 600 engine. The trio were to prove unreliable and so became the last heavy Leylands purchased by Smiths who turned to buying ERF, Foden and Atkinson tractor units. Seen hauling a BTC 4 in line semi-trailer, the well turned out tractor bore chassis number 611824 and was regularly driven by Joe Scott who in turn was well known for his meticulous way of working.

The out of sequence fleet number indicates that this 1964 two stroke powered Commer was not a Smiths owned vehicle. Although the company fleet size was to peak around the 130 mark, they also made great use of sub contractors and owner drivers - some of whom painted their vehicles in Smith's colours. This eight ton capacity four wheeler belonged to Sam Neale Transport - later to become a director at Smiths. Regular driver of the Maxiload was Eddie Morris, a former Salford tram driver. Amongst other regular sub contractors to Smiths were Bostocks of Congleton, who are currently well known for their immaculate fleet of mature ERFs and Atkinsons.

H Evers was another Manchester company with a long history, Harry Evers starting off with horses in 1916. Harry eventually retired to South Africa and the company passed into the Transport Development Group via Settle Speakman. After a couple of years the Ancoats premises were sold and the mixed fleet of 27 tippers added to the Smiths of Eccles operation whilst retaining the Evers name. Photographed by Roger Kenny, 7334 VU was part of that 1972 transfer although the short wheelbase to this '63 Foden meant it was still being ran at 24 tons gross.

Smiths had always been able to haul abnormal loads up to the 25 ton mark but in 1975 they increased their capability by taking over the Walter Denton operation - whilst still retaining the 1886 name. Six Foden winch tractors - all ballast box units - plus 20 trailers were to come to Taylor Road, with perhaps the best remembered of these being TMB 843D which had the Gardner 6LX-150 engine and 12 speed double underdrive gearbox. Although it only had a top speed of 25 mph, it's tremendous pulling power was put to the test when it had to recover the fully loaded Denton six wheeler. At an all up weight of 117 tons, this diminutive Foden did the recovery with ease.

Staverton Builders big low loader of 1950 was this Gardner powered ERF-BTC outfit which like the rest of the fleet was painted dark green with gold lettering. Driver Ted King is cleaning the winter dirt from his headlights at Narborough, Leicestershire whilst the photographer - and driver's mate - was Norman Cleave. Enroute from the Ruston Bucyrus factory at Lincoln with a brand new 10RB excavator, the crew were only able to get as far back as Bridgewater. The Suez crisis of 1956 meant they were unable to buy any fuel on the road and they had to wait on the A38 until diesel was brought up from Totnes HQ. This 6LW engined low loader was expected to haul all the company's plant - the heaviest being a 22RB - around any of their south west building sites. Geared down to a modest 23 mph still didn't impress Somerset traffic police as they insisted that the ERF only did 12 mph and required that a plate be fitted on the back of the trailer to so indicate.

Created via the efforts of the Elmhurst family of Dartington Hall, Staverton took their name from a small village just north of Totnes. Like many in the building trade at that time, Staverton made use of an assortment of general work horses including Fordson 7V tippers with V8 petrol engines - agony to start on a wet morning - along with an Albion which wasn't even fitted with an electric starter. Seven petrol engined O series Bedfords in use were rated as 4-5 tonners although at times they carried twice this weight. Norman Cleave was driving this Edbro equipped tipper which is pictured in 1955 on excavation work at an old airfield near Taunton. Staverton's distinctive trademark - used on the company's vehicles, plant and stationery - was the Egyptian hieroglyph "Ankh", which meant the key of life.

John Thomas currently heads the 66 strong high profile fleet of Ken Thomas Ltd which has it's HQ on Thorney Road at Guyhirn. The family owned concern trace their roots back to grandfather David Thomas who worked out of Pear Tree Farm at Guyhirn. As a fenland farmer he made use of this A series Ford as a workhorse during the late 1930s and it's seen carrying an impressive load of chaff. As well as being used in the production of animal feed, the rather light sackfuls were utilised as bedding for the Irish land workers who came to the Fens in the picking season.

Ken Thomas was to follow his father into the mix of farming and transport business when he set up on his own during 1948 on an eight acre plot situated 300 yards away from the parental home, down the A47. Ken's first two vehicles were ex WD Bedfords driven by Dougie Watson and Harry Marchington. They were to be used on produce traffic mainly to deliver into Birmingham and London markets in the early hours. The first diesel engined vehicle to enter the Thomas fleet was this Dodge, BEG 469. Dating from 1951, the four wheeler ran with canvas tilt type bodywork when strawberries and other soft fruit were in season. For normal vegetable produce it was ran in dropside form.

Opposite: As Ken expanded, he wanted to set up a pull in for other drivers so in 1953 he used two army huts to form the basis of a cafe. Ken's wife Joyce - always known as Jo - ran this well patronised establishment which was named 'Coronation' because of thc big royal event held in that year. Obviously well liked by Midlands based Tarmac wagons, the cafe was famous because of it's opening hours. During the week these were 7am-7pm but on Friday and Saturday nights it served until 2am when even Ken found himself behind the counter. The Coronation was ran by Jo until it closed in 1989.

First painting his vehicles green, Ken adopted a red livery in 1962 the year when he took on limited status. The fleet line up at that point showed a predominance of TK Bedford rigids - the vehicle fourth from the right was their sole artic - which were supplied new through Murketts who had outlets at Peterborough and Huntingdon. Ken adopted a policy of replacing these Bedfords when they were exactly a year old so that apart from the regular servicing, any repairs involved were covered by the vehicle's warranty. When trading in the year old vehicle, it apparently cost Thomas' £365 for a new one - in other words, each Bedford cost the company a £1 a day to operate. The sole 1962 Dodge - which was supplied through Peterborough Engineers - was Derek Tyler's vehicle, a driver who's still with Thomas' in 1994.

By 1958, Thomas' had expanded to this line up of eight. The two Austins in the centre had been bought specifically for their carriers licences although the preference of a Dodge and Bedford mix was still to the fore. The Dodge on the left was the company's first artic and it was usually driven by George Bowles. Daily runs to the market with produce was still the main form of traffic with the two S type Bedfords on the right being loaded with carrots. The third Bedford was loaded with meal, this being collected from BOCM at Wisbech for delivery to the local farms. These S types were the first new vehicles bought by Thomas. During late April and May each year when produce work went quiet, the drivers removed all the vehicle bodies for chassis painting prior to the busy season ahead.

In 1966 Thomas' had their first 12,000 sq ft warehouse built at the Old Station Yard and seen in the photograph are Dick Moyses on the fork lift with driver John Wakeling. Delivering Chivers Hartley produce into store, the two stroke powered Commer Maxiload was one of two similar artics which were fitted with the Scammell automatic coupling. In 1966 Thomas' also ran two Commer four wheeled rigids and two Maxiload fifth wheel artics - FJE 951D and GEB 197E. The company were to expand their warehousing to it's current level of 140,000 sq ft.

In 1968 Ken Thomas changed his livery again to the company's current cream, green and red mix. It was prompted after Ken had taken over the 12 strong fleet and work load - but not the business name - of Fenland Transport Services which had been ran in these colours. The purchase from John Briggs went through on January 2, 1968, the vehicles bought including four Guys - JJE 78, LEB 30, MEG 125 and YOF 927 - a Deutz - LFL 674F, two Scammells - MXV 394 and FFL 647D - plus an Atkinson artic unit FXY 918 which had started life as a rigid. Although the Fenland transaction prompted the creation of a second depot at Thorney, the old vehicles were soon moved on as ERFs were favoured - the 6LW powered JVE 660F being the first of the marque into service. This line up was used on the company's South Wales trunk, the Crane Fruehauf van pictured being for a specific canned work contract where the customer didn't want his load sheeted.

Although Ken Thomas was a big fan of the Gardner 6LX-180 engine, over demand from other hauliers meant most of the late '60s ERF tractor units came with the Cummins 205 engine. Doug Hudson is the smiling face at the wheel of NEB 302H which was supplied new through the Sellers & Batty dealership. Being carried on the York Teamster semi-trailer is one of the many loads of castings which Thomas' carried on behalf of their Peterborough manufacturer, Baker Perkins. While ERF no longer figures strongly in the current fleet, one of the latest vehicles of the growing Thomas Vintage collection is 430 DYD, a 1959 ERF KV tractor unit which started life with Showerings of Shepton Mallett.

During the 1960s all manner of vehicles were tried by Thomas' and three Leyland Badgers are recalled as going that fast, the fan blades regularly used to come off. The company traded these in to Peterborough Engineering and in their place came three Foden S39 tractor units. Seen with the new vehicles at Thorney are - left to right - Dougie Watson (Ken's first driver), Michael Thomas, Ken Thomas and Joe Singleterry who started with the company as a driver and ended up as transport manager. Michael Thomas currently runs his own business at Thorney whilst Ken Thomas was to die in 1983.

In the first half of this century, Vineys grew to become one of the greatest names in transport operating in England's north west. Founded in 1906, the business was actually created to develop the Viney steam wagon which had been patented by Horace Viney. Circumstances however prevented the concept going much further and as an alternative, the company turned it's interests to road haulage buying their first of two Coulthards in that year. Joining Vineys on December 1, 1906, was Mr C le M Gosselin who was to take over the business - but retain

the Viney name - in 1908. Steam still played an important part in the Viney story and they strongly favoured the Leyland product although during the 1920s exceptions to this preference were an Aveling & Porter 5 tonner, a Tasker steam tractor and a Garrett tractor. Leyland fleet number 32 was used until it's final excise licence expired during 1926.

In total, Vineys were to operate 34 Leyland steamers - although not all at the same time - between 1907, when they first arrived and 1934. Unlike their petrol and later diesel powered vehicles, the Leyland production of steamers - which ran until the early 1920s - was comparitively small when compared to the likes of Foden and Sentinel. Those numbers that were made usually ended up being operated in Lancashire. CK 458 is a class F Leyland steam wagon which was new in 1912 and Alan Martin's research records that it was ran by Vineys until it was scapped in 1934.

Opposite: Vineys soon developed a reputation for being able to haul most things for most men. Produced by the Lytham Shipbuilding and Engineering Co Ltd, this vessel was destined for delivery into Preston docks. The shipbuilder's products reached all parts of the globe and they are believed responsible for many of the paddle steamers which worked the Mississipi in the USA. Nearer to home, one of their last vessels was the "James Duke" which until 1990 ferried passangers and cars across Lake Windermere. Leyland fleet number 8 was registered B 2103.

Below: With Vineys being based in Strand Road at Preston, it wasn't surprising they hauled the products of their near neighbours. Dick Kerr was another well respected name in Preston's industrial heritage, Messers Dick and Kerr combining in the factory that produced all manner of electrical items. Destined for Liverpool Corporation, Vineys hauled the Dick Kerr trams in partially knocked down condition. Leyland steamer CK 467 was new in 1913 and kept in service at Vineys until it was scrapped in 1933.

Although Vineys operated generally in Lancashire and the adjacent counties, they depended for a considerable portion of their traffic on the port of Preston, whose famous Albert Edward dock was opened in 1892. Better known for handling cargo rather than passengers, it specialised in receiving traffic from the Baltic and Scandinavia as it was rated as being the seventh most important port in the UK for timber imports. Hauling such a load is CK 3192, the petrol engined QH2 Leyland four wheeler dating from 1926.

Whilst most of Vineys vehicles were painted in the company's normal colours (green, green & black or green & red), the road tanker division usually found themselves painted in a dedicated customer's colours. In 1925 Vineys formed the subsidiary concern of Lancashire Petrol Deliveries Ltd primarily to deal with deliveries of petrol and other light hydrocarbon oils. The Texaco liveried Leyland pictured around 1926 sports a two compartment tank with a capacity of 1,000 gallons. The five Leyland QH2 petrol engined vehicles seen about 1927 have 1500 gallon tanks split into three compartments. ROP - Russian Oil Products - was a large national producer in this period with another famous tanker concern, Crow Carrying Company, running some vehicles in ROP colours to service the London area in the late 1920s.

In 1928 Leyland began to adopt animal names for their models although CK 3743 was simply coded as a petrol engined SQ2. Seen about 1930, Vineys had been forced to adapt their tram carrying roadtrains to the larger product being made by Dick Kerr. The tram however, was a rather modest product of this manufacturer who went on to make washing machines and even the famous Canberra bomber. Although Dick Kerrs were to evolve into English Electric, the current link with GEC Alsthom now has the Preston staff making traction engines for the modern day generation of trams.

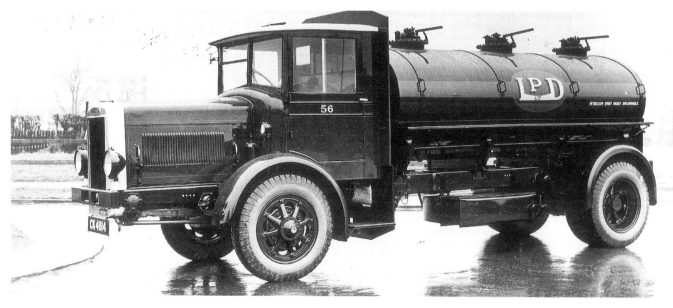

CK 4614 was chassis number 134, the Leyland Buffalo being sold to Vineys in November 1931. The 1500 gallon tanker had it's front axle set back to improve axle loadings - a problem even in those early days - but the layout's recalled as not being entirely successful as it took too much weight. By 1940 LPD were running 35 tankers and by 1949 this had increased to 53. Vineys sold out voluntarily to the Road Haulage Executive (tankers were exempt from compulsory nationalisation) around October 1, 1949, their HQ at 65, Water Lane, Preston being first known as Unit C.52, but then becoming Preston's main BRS depot. Viney/LPD were then operating vehicles from depots in Liverpool, Bromborough, Urmston and Ancoats. Although the name of Vineys did not re-emerge in the early '50s phase of de-nationalisation, the Gosselins were set to head south for Thames valley and create another famous name in the heritage of road tanker operation.

It was in 1919 when brothers Walter and Bernard Viney set themselves up as hauliers in the Somerset town of Bruton. The partnership wasn't to last however as Bernard decided to follow other interests but Walter was soon joined by two of his nephews - Jim Viney and Tom Amblin - who are pictured with this six wheeled Foden R type YD 4764. New in 1933, fleet number 9 was Vineys first Foden diesel as fleet number 8 - YD 1771 - had been one of Fodens last O type steamers - also a six wheeled dropsider. Written on the rear facing tailgate of the Fodens was the grand wording 'Estimates Free - Satisfaction Guaranteed'.

Jim Viney soon showed a natural flair in engineering and as well as being responsible for all the fleet repairs, he took on the job of deciding which new vehicles would be purchased. Although they were normally sourced from the Cheshire town of Sandbach, Jim visited both ERF and Foden factories before deciding which marque to buy. Jim is stood with one of Vineys first ERFs, YD 8810 dating from 1934. Maintained in their own workshops, during the mid 1930s Vineys yard was also used as the local weekly cattle market. Also coming into service during the '30s were Morris Commercials AYA 618, AYB 703 and BYC 377 whilst AYC 143 was a four wheeled Albion.

Although Vineys did a lot of general haulage work - they even did a daily collection of the Royal Mail from Evercreech Junction - the natural resources of the surrounding Mendip hills meant tippers were in great demand. AYC 623 was new in 1935, the ERF sporting a three way tipping body. This six wheeler had been sold on before Vineys were nationalised on June 2, 1948. The 17 strong fleet being operated at the time - which became Unit F78 - included 11 tippers. Fodens were strongly favoured then with 3 four wheelers: EYA 712, CYD 173 and LYA 724 plus 3 eight wheelers: CYD 386, HYA 83 and LYA 324. There was a Guy 5 ton tipper HYB 488, two similar Bedfords EYD 38 and GYA 484 whilst FYB 762 was a Vulcan four wheeler.

In 1955, 14 ex BRS vehicles - and the old Viney yard - were bought to put W Viney Ltd back on the haulage scene. Rather than adopt the old colours - a striking red with black chassis - which were very similar to those of BRS, the new fleet was painted green. Many of the old driving staff like Stan Vincent, brothers Lobby and Cyril Jeffries, Reg Weeks and Eric Mainstone also came back to work at Vineys. Although Walter Viney died in 1956, his two nephews - Jim is pictured with this 1959 Albion Reiver - expanded the business until their deaths in the mid 1960s. Merged into the William Nuttall Transport Group in 1969, Vineys were to loose their identity when Nuttalls became part of the Renwick Group about 1973. However it's quite fitting that a housing estate built in Bruton on the site of the old Viney premises has been named Vineys Yard.

Henry Whiteway was one of the earliest commercial producers of Devonshire 'cyder', in 1903 his Whimple factory - just east of Exeter - was making 130,000 gallons a year. A distribution network was established and by the 1950s, the long distance Devonshire vehicles were serving depots in London, Pershore and Sheffield as well as up into Scotland's central belt. This trio, pictured on the Exeter by pass in 1959, was part of the nine strong fleet working out of the company's Abbotskerrswell depot near Newton Abbot. Whilst long serving driver Eric Bann is seen in the Atkinson six wheeler, the standing figure is Henry Bicknell who drove the leading Dennis Pax. Norman Cleave's similar Dennis - YUO 474 - takes up the rear, the four wheeler being recalled for a rather sluggish Perkins P6 engine but giving a comfortable and reliable performance.

Whiteways first produced the long running Cydrax as 'the great temperance drink' in 1903. Peardrax, a soft drink made from pear juice, was first marketed in 1957 but the company was also famous for their Cyder vinegar and the fact they produced Sanatogen tonic wine - albeit under licence. The road fleet had a similar mix to the products they were carrying but all were painted in duck egg blue with red lettering and yellow bodies. NDV 596 was Whiteways only Atky six wheeler and new in 1952, the Gardner 6LW powered vehicle would normally be seen driven by Eric Bann on his once a week round trip between Newton Abbot and Glasgow at a top speed of 33 mph. The fairly short body length was a Whiteway spec' because if the vehicle had been any longer, it wouldn't have been able to make the entrance of Dunns, a regular Glasgow drop. After Eric's seven year stint with the vehicle, Norman Cleave took it over in 1959.

Whiteways Whimple depot was to strongly favour the Guy Otter as a 6-7 tonner for multi drop work in the south west and Wales. With a mixture of Perkins P6 or Gardner 4LK engines, some of the older Otters had Meadows petrol engines and were deemed not to need anti-freeze. Each driver was issued with a watering can and instructed to drain off the radiator every winter's night. When parked overnight away from the depot it was a company instruction to the Guy drivers to remove the indian's head radiator cap, in case it was stolen. The company's first artic was an Albion Chieftan with the Dodge 638 CTA coming new in 1959. A Leyland Comet engine and Turner gearbox driving an Eaton two speed axle combined to give a good performance although the pictured regular driver Maurice Ellis said it never steered quite right. Whiteways drivers reckoned the narrow track of the front axle was adopted because manufacturer Dodge had some old Kew axles in stock which they wanted to use up.

Whiteways always had a long standing interest in overseas markets and in recent times were shipping 500,000 gallons to Trinidad and the West Indies. This connection with sunnier climes contrasts with Norman Cleave's situation in the winter of 1962 on the A702 between Abington and Biggar with a full load of 'Pony' wine bound for Edinburgh. Eric Whiteway, who ran the company transport, had always said, "You don't need a heater in the cab, it's already got an engine in there", as to the reason why none of the older vehicles were fitted with heaters. Driver Cleave reports that thankfully this option was a standard fit to his Dodge and it was also the first company vehicle to come with power steering. Norman received the Perkins 6.354 engined 9 tonner in 1961, the year when Whiteways merged with Showerings and Vine Products to form SVW. This group was later to be absorbed into the Allied Lyons organisation.

Mark Whitton was a farmer of Cullompton in Devon who began in haulage during the early 1900s using a horse and cart on timber work. His sons Reg, Wilfred and Harold were to expand into the mechanised age with AW 8624 proudly displaying the fleet number 1. Pictured on the left is Jack Wright who spent all his working life at Whittons. The Sentinel was a 6 tonner it being works number 3619 of 1920 vintage. Other Sentinels ran by Whittons were TA 9338, TT 7210 - fleet number 6 being a tipper - and fleet number 8, UO 2317, another tipper which hauled a drawbar trailer.

By 1935, Whittons were leaving the steam era behind and they took delivery of two Leyland Beavers - fleet number 26 being BUO 67 - with both of them hauling a Carrimore drawbar trailer. Their Duralloy body was of a Whitton spec' intended to carry loads of paper although the high sides also proved ideal to support barrels of cider. Fred Radford was 25's usual driver and his normal route was the trunk to London. The limitations of the Abbots Kerswell Cider Co at Newton Abbot didn't allow enough space for a wagon and drag so the trailers had to be left in the Whitton yard and their loads transhipped onto them. 26 was later sold into fairground service whilst 25 was converted into an articulated tractor unit.

AOD 955 was chassis number 0386120 and is believed to have been the first AEC Mammoth Major eight wheeler into service in Devon. It's cab was built by Lee Motors of Winton, Bournemouth and it sports the optional sun visor plus illuminated headboard which has been blacked out as a war time requirement. Regularly driven by Bill Jolliffe, this AEC plus another Whitton eight wheeler - DUO 446 - were two of about 100 AECs which went to Holland at the end of the war and spent about three months ferrying foodstuffs from the north sea ports to inland towns. Other AECs which featured in the first Whitton fleet were EDV 496, EOJ 102 and HOD 752 - all six wheelers - and the eight wheeler KDV 449. Two early Mandator tractor units were KTA 540 and KUO 181. The company's sole Leyland Octopus eight wheeler was CTJ 179, which was bought second hand in the early 1940s.

In June 1949, Whittons were running a 40 strong general haulage fleet which was compulsorily nationalised. In some respects it was business as usual with Reg being the BRS depot manager at Cullompton and Harold high up on the engineering side (Wilfred had left in the '30s to set up a dairy business). Harold especially, however, couldn't wait to become his own boss once more so in 1955 the brothers bought two S type Bedford artics - fleet number 24 was EPR 269 - ex BRS Poole to start up again. A batch of 20 furthur vehicles came from BRS Watchet and although they were of a questionable variety, it was the carriers licences attached to them which were of the main importance. Pictured here are left to right: URF 127 - fleet number 44 and registered as a Maudslay; JXK 366 - fleet number 42, a petrol engined Albion FT3; MEL 171 - an ex BRS Watchet vehicle driven by Reg Tooze and MLK 34 - fleet number 36 - which together with MXD 77 came ex Wimpey.

With the Road Haulage Executive retaining title to the original Whittons Transport Ltd name, the brothers were obliged to register themselves differently. When still working for BRS, they had bought a local bus operation called Green & Cream Coaches Ltd. This five strong fleet was never a great success although it gave the name to coin Whittons Green & Cream Ltd. YUO 915 was new in 1958, the AEC Mercury tractor unit being coupled to a York semi-trailer and sporting a cab built by Oldland Motor Bodies of Bristol. Joe Wilson was the artic's usual driver and it's load of paper could incorporate 15 drops in Scotland - a full week's work. Like the similar Mercury rigid WUO 215, the new AECs were bought by Whittons through AECs south west representative Bob Sykes who lived at Exmouth.

In 1966 Whittons Heavy Haulage Ltd was created with a base in Exeter. With five low loaders - plus a number of mobile cranes - this part of Whittons was ran by John Cruwys who had been with Pickfords at Exeter until that branch had closed. Seen at Pocombe Bridge in 1967, the yacht 'Sundancer' was built by Len Last in a barn on Eastwood Farm. Moving it the five miles to the City Basin in Exeter took the expertise of driver Cyril Simmons and the strangest of outfits. Seen with a cap in the centre of shot is Wally Woodhall who built the step frame semi-trailer and the six wheeled bogie (which started life as an Atkinson). Although 'Heavy Haulage' performed reasonably well, some aspects of Whittons diversification were to create cash flow problems in the early 1970s. In 1973 the company ceased trading when they were acquired by the Wild Group of Exeter.

In pre BRS days the Whittons vehicles were painted chocolate brown although with the new title, the colours of green and cream were taken into use. 720 HYB sports the second version to the new livery although this 1960 Guy Warrior Light 8 was bought second hand. The Whitton brothers had long been very weight conscious and had always bought their eight wheeled Mammoth Majors with single drive bogies so the Light 8 was preferred to the similar, but heavier, Guy Invincible. Mark Cox was this tipper's normal driver, it usually spending it's time carrying bulk grain between Avonmouth docks and the mills around Tiverton.

Although both brothers were involved in returning Whittons to private enterprise, Reg felt he was too old to re-join the fray and stayed with BRS until his retirement. Harold was to bring his two sons - Martin and Graham - into the business which expanded to the 80 mark. Transport Manager at Whittons was Dick Bradbeer who took time out to ensure the Whitton vehicles were photographed for posterity. 653 HTT dates from 1961, the Leyland engined Dodge being supplied new through Coventry & Jeffs of Bristol. Found to be too heavy in it's original four wheeled form, Whittons sent it to Primrose for a second steer axle to be added. Drivers like Nicky Armstrong who cut their teeth on this chinese six recall it for heavy steering, a willing heart but questionable brakes.